To Barbara ~
May your photos delight
and amaze you!

　　　　　～Christi

　　　　　12.3.15

FOCUS

FOCUS

Finding the Hidden Messages
in Your Personal Photographs

Christi Koelker

Lucky Valley Press
Jacksonville, Oregon & Carmel, California

Published by Lucky Valley Press
Jacksonville, Oregon & Carmel, California
WWW.LUCKYVALLEYPRESS.COM

Printed in the United States of America
on paper produced through sustainable forestry practices.

DEDICATION

To all the people in my life who have believed in my vision
even when I doubted it.

I'm grateful every day for the gift of each one of you.

Medrith Ann Saxon

George Saxon, Jr.

Candice Barley

Brooks Barley

Jamie Koelker

Leanne Barley

Kathryn Bowman

CONTENTS

INTRODUCTION/PROLOGUE

"My snapshots and photos have messages for me? How is that possible?"

Shapes, symbols, forms, and colors talk to our intuitive brain. The side that doesn't speak in words. Sometimes our intuitive brain (the part that recognizes overall concepts without having to figure them out) gets pushed to the side. We're creatures of reason. Maybe I should say that we become creatures of reason. We're not necessarily born that way.

We enter this world and spend about the first five years in a state of divine connectedness to our physical beings and the basic desires we inherently want in the moment. We don't spend our time trying to reason out why we want and do what we do—we just know.

Slowly, we learn to turn off that primary communication link. Or we re-tune the frequency to one that seems to serve us better as humans who possess the most obvious five senses (taste, smell, hearing, touch, and sight). The point at which we lose our connection with that incredibly important transmission is when at least half of our communication system withers. Our personal GPS no longer functions with its full capabilities. We start to feel that we've lost our bearings.

And even though we can't really put our fingers on the reason, we feel an uneasiness. We aren't fluent anymore in our most basic individual language. Although we attempt to squelch it, often silently so as not to concern our companions, we can't completely quiet the echo of a powerful influence trying to express itself in our lives, especially during our first few years here. It's constantly nudging at the back of our brains for our acknowledgement. In fleeting dreams, it floods our minds with images that we can only dimly recall in the light of day. It's inside our throats causing us to hum a vague string of notes we don't consciously recognize as belonging to any song we've heard.

It's drawing our eyes to one particular word on a newspaper page filled with thousands of other words. We witness ourselves as we stop reading the story and stare at one, single word. It feels strange. We don't rationally know why we're doing it. We only know we "recognize" something about it that's deeply, profoundly familiar.

The early peoples had their shamans, medicine men, curanderas, omen readers and divination experts who "read" everything from the flights of birds to the cycles of the moon. Today, we have come to rely on our "properly" licensed psychiatrists and physicians, chemists and pharmacists (as informed by the mega-drug corporations), preachers and priests to scrutinize our physical and psychical dis–eases. We then pin our hopes on the promise that a single pill will fix whatever is out of whack whether or not we can discern its origin. We pray we'll soon be able to get back on the roller coaster (back in the saddle, back in the game) again to ride the tracks once more without the annoying, and frequently painful, downtime.

The adage, "You can't know where you're going unless you know where you've been" is applicable here. I'd massage it to proclaim: You can't know who you are—or are capable of becoming—unless you've focused on who you've been in historical time in concert with all of timeless creation at your side. Those stories are in your personal photographs, particularly your snapshots.

You can witness the language that was embedded in you and has been communicating with you for this lifetime and, some would claim, for all eternity. Since we live in an age of advanced technology, when the camera is an integral aspect of our everyday existence, for the first time we have the opportunity to get an in depth picture of who we truly are. The precise moment in time has arrived for us to be the pioneers who will travel inward with our own version of our personal Hubble Space Telescope (HST).[1]

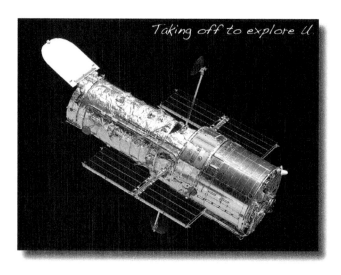

Taking off to explore U.

Individually, we are certainly as complicated as the vast universe the HST explores. With (give or take) 37.2 trillion cells in our body,[2] we are each an entire universe unto ourselves. Our experts (of the scientific persuasion) assure us with each new year that we are infinitely complex. But each of us has to go alone into that vast inner landscape by ourselves because we're the only ones who can interpret the meaning of our personal symbols. It would take another lifetime to explain them to anyone else even if they were capable of setting aside all of their interpretations and perceptions of their own lives while we took the many years required to explained ours.

Nobody else has the time or energy to investigate us. Not really. Not in the entirety it takes to completely understand the intricacies that comprise each individual's spirit. So we assume it's of no value to anybody else, maybe not even to ourselves. We take our individual communication systems for granted as they fuel our personal lexicon. The codex is arranged in a sequence that only we can access. We talk to ourselves every day, perhaps every waking moment, in our own internal language that has its etymology in the linguistics of our personal experiences. Since this is a solitary process and we are generally a very busy race, we don't honor our unique language or even much value it as singular in the world. We spend most of our lives attempting to access everyone else's internal dictionary so we can love them, sell them or understand them.

The premise of this book is that, if we take some time to focus inward and begin to decipher our own codex of meaning, only then can we honor and comprehend the depths of any other person's journey and, in turn, their experiences. Only when we figure out the significance of our own symbology can we possibly understand how one color, one shape, one image, one sound or one smell can be the root of a whole realm of perception in another human's world.

And so, we will begin our journey to plot our inner space probe mission by looking for the messages waiting for us in our old photos and snapshots. Those are the first places we'll begin digging for clues to unlock our very personal inner vocabulary.

Chapter Notes:
1. HST-SM4 [Photograph]. (2009). Retrieved October 3, 2014, from: http://commons.wikimedia.org/wiki/File:HST-SM4.jpeg.
2. Eveleth, Rose. (2013, October 24). There Are 37.2 Trillion Cells in Your Body. Retrieved from http://www.smithsonianmag.com/smart-news/there-are-372-trillion-cells-in-your- body-4941473/?no-ist.

PART ONE: THE ANSWER IS IN OUR IMAGES

"Trying to understand what's happening using old words, old images, old paradigms is like telling time by broken clocks. The landscape created by speech, writing, print is being terraformed by digital humans, rocking in our boots, out of joint with our times. We are riding a ship on the river of time as the ship is being built. It will take time to finish that ship, and when we do, we will already have been becoming something else." [3]

Richard Thieme

In the 1980s, Episcopal priest Richard Thieme started publishing his visions of the future and predicted the influence of the evolving technologies on religion and individual spirituality. In less than 30 years, his "radical" ideas are accepted as common sense by mainstream, non-philosophical types of folks. Thieme states, "The truth of whatever is 'out there' is fused to the symbols by which we sense its presence in our lives. Time is simultaneously tamed and made sacred, organized in a way that lets us share a story and also believe that the story is about What's Really So."[4]

There has simply never been any time in recorded history that's comparable to the 20th and 21st centuries. Industry and technology have evolved at such a breakneck speed and at such a jet-propelled pace that this spinning orb on which we live is hardly recognizable as the same planet from only 150 years ago. One could argue, and many do, about the pros and cons of this radically fast trajectory of change. Regardless of what any one expert or woman on the street thinks, change has come and it's going to keep on 'a coming for quite a while. In fact, change may be the one constant on which we can depend.

In the year of 1826 or '27, the first permanent photograph was produced by the French inventor Joseph Nicéphore Niépce. Plenty of other people throughout history were interested in capturing inside a box what they witnessed in the outside world. Many toyed with primitive ideas; other curious enthusiasts and early scientists dabbled with the enigmatic camera obscura. It was used by certain painters to help them to render subjects with more realism and written about as long ago as the fifth century BC. But by the 19th and 20th centuries, people became almost obsessed with the idea of being able to capture their images on film.

The image above, on the left, is a close-up copy of Niépce's first photograph. It's entitled *View From the Window at Le Gras*. This copy was enhanced in the early 1950s to show the detail. The photo next to it is of me visiting the actual image at its permanent home (nestled in a darkened alcove) in the Harry Ransom Center at the University of Texas, Austin.[5] This is the original plate, held inside a frame, that was captured in the 1820s on a 20 x 25 cm (approximately 7 x 9 inch) silver plate coated with oil-treated bitumen. Bitumen is somewhat similar to tar.

At present, in the early part of the 21st century, photography, filmmaking, video and personal visual expression are more widely practiced than ever. Future generations will be able to witness their ancestor's births as it was captured on some form of digital media hundreds of years before. Sharing those familial images at gatherings and reunions will be as normal as opening our scrapbooks today.

The ability of people, without any special training in cinematography or photography, to document their lives and commit it to a visual medium will most definitely (in fact already has) change the way history is perceived. From this moment forward, history is permanently recorded and uploaded to the Internet for anyone to view and judge for themselves. That's what those who come after us will rely on more than individual teachers or textbooks. We can't predict exactly what people will use for technology, but we do know that our relationship with the Internet and the proliferation of sites like YouTube and Vimeo have forever altered the way we access, process and interpret our information.

The essence and the heart of using a visual medium (photography, film, etc.) enables us to do something quite magical. It imbues us with the power to actually perform what science fiction authors H. G. Wells, Ray Bradbury and Rod Serling only imagined in their fantastic stories. It functions as a literal time machine.

We live in what mathematicians and physicists call the "third dimension." Frequently, time is referred to as the "fourth dimension." Science fiction stories are full of extraordinary tales of alternate dimensions, parallel universes and other planes of existence. In most instances, the time traveler must visit these places by slipping into a spatial direction not experientially proven heretofore. In a number of stories, these other universes and planes correspond with the three-dimensional one we inhabit during our waking hours. The distance to be traversed to enter these other worlds is not up or down or sideways or back and forth.

It's through.

The majority of us believe we can't navigate around in time and are bound to move in only one direction: the future. Yet, we indeed time travel by entering through the present moment and sliding into an image.

Consider for a moment what happens when we intensely focus on a photograph or a movie. We become so fixated by the images that we literally lose ourselves inside of it—even if only for a moment. We are there. On the interior. Where the image is now and where it was captured. We can even hear what was going on just off camera. We smell the fragrance or the stench. We feel the love or the hate or the tension or the joy. All those sensations are real to us merely for a split second, but we are literally, physically there.

Are we transported "through" time and into some outpost or territory of the fourth dimension? We definitely experience that we're within the image we're involved in for some part of a moment. Everybody who's ever thumbed through a magazine or watched a movie would admit that they've had that type of "time suspension" or "time travel" experience. It wasn't scary and it didn't require the crazy contraption Rod Taylor was riding in the 1960 film, *The Time Machine*. It was easy. It was safe. No Morlocks oozed out of the walls to eat us.

When we look closely at a photographic image, it enables us to stop time, engage intensely with an instant, gain back a moment and expand it from within our own space/time until we have absorbed the information contained in it. This ability is a relatively contemporary operation for our brains. Yes, painters took an event and suspended it in time, but not necessarily a moment that occurred in reality. More like a personal impression that's been Photoshopped as it's being created for the first time or their interpretation of a scene.

I fervently believe that photography, and our passionate devotion to the visual duplicates (or creation or replication) of particular moments, entered history precisely when it did because the elements it brought along with it were essential to us. We, as co-creative humans, needed the camera and the images produced by it to advance in our scientific and spiritual growth. Being physically able to suspend events, places, people or things until we can find the time to examine them, process them in more detail and integrate what we observe into our lives are traits that we were destined to develop in order to function in the multi-dimensional, multi-tasking world that evolved right alongside it.

Here's one scenario of why we might not be able to process much of what happens to us, with us and for us in one 24-hour period.

It's entirely possible (and is no surprise to most of us) that you can awaken on a particular morning in the heart of New York City, grab a bagel on the way to the airport, hop a five hour flight to San Diego (where you magically gain back three hours, making it a 27 hour day), rent a car, and drive to La Jolla for a bite at The Marine Room, where the turquoise waves of the Pacific Ocean lap against the glass windows. Then, you can get back in the car and drive south to the Mexico-United States border, where you'll get caught in the honking and yelling drivers of Tijuana. After you weather that, you'll find a friendly mercado to rummage through cubby holes for colorful trinkets. Finally, you'll scoot back to the airport, take a flight to Victoria to enjoy a beautiful dinner at the charming Café Brio before turning in at a lovely British Columbian inn.

Although I tracked the day by destination and food (world travel and local food are two of my personal passions) the intensity of any one of these experiences for, let's say, a 19th century farmer is immense. His or her survival depended on how well a seed sprouted and if the weather was cooperative enough to deliver the perfect blend of rain and sun to effectively harvest.

Indeed, there are still plenty of people in the world who farm and don't jet all over North America in a single day. In fact, most of us don't ever experience that kind of whirlwind lifestyle. But the possibility exists for almost any of us to spend a day of our lives being transported from location to location. And we, as a civilization, accept this so easily into our collective consciousness that it's sort of mundane to even discuss it.

The aim of this illustration is to bring attention to the inherent difficulty of tracking and keeping up with valuable pieces of yourself which are lost inside the events of your life. They occur faster than your mind can process them. To our inner selves, it's like living life on a roller coaster. Events, people, places and feelings all rush by our faces like the wind as we plummet down the tracks and hang onto the safety bar in the coaster. If the jetsetter described before failed to make some sort of documentation of her day, how much of what she saw, ate and experienced could be "digested" into her consciousness? She couldn't possibly see it all or take it in at once. It's not humanly possible.

Photographs, especially the ones that don't make it into the albums or the frames on your shelves, are particularly powerful pictographs of your intuitive life. They're the touchstones you've gathered of your inner vocabulary. Although you may have intended to document the birthday party of your one-year-old or your visit to the Grand Canyon, there was far more recorded than you realized as you inadvertently pointed your camera a little to the left or your hands shook slightly, causing the picture to snap with the lens pointed more skyward.

Obviously, every old photo stuffed in the back of a drawer or on a shelf in the top of a closet is not going to yield an image deserving of study. Some are just dark, out-of-focus, unfortunate wastes of paper and time. But others will yield a clue or two about what was happening around and inside of you at the instant the shutter blinked.

The process for determining which of these images rates more than a second look is the subject of the rest of this book.

Chapter Notes:

3. R. Thieme. (1998, November 28). *Telling Time By a Broken Clock* (Web log comment). Retrieved from http://www.thiemeworks.com/telling-time-by-a-broken-clock/.

4. Ibid.

5. *View from the Window at Le Gras*, Joseph Nicéphore Niépce.jpg [Photograph]. (1825 or 1827). Retrieved October 3, 2014 from http://en.wikipedia.org/wiki/File:View_from_the_Window_at_Le_Gras,_Joseph_Nic%C3%A9phore_Ni%C3%A9pce.jpg.

Enhanced version by the Swiss Helmut Gersheim (1913–1995), performed ca. 1952, of Niépce's *View from the Window at Le Gras*, (Harry Ransom Humanities Research Center, University of Texas, Austin).

6. [On Page 3.] Poster for the film: *The Time Machine* (1960 film) [Photograph]. (1960). Retrieved October 3, 2014, from http://commons.wikimedia.org/wiki/File:Brown,r_time_macine60.jpg.

IMAGES ARE ENERGY!

"Death signifies nothing. The distinction between past, present and future is only a stubbornly persistent illusion."

Albert Einstein shortly before his own death in 1955

"In the permanence of space-time, the idea that this moment exists somewhere in the universe: everybody makes a mark in space-time. I think one of the things that Einstein was telling us with that quote and with his theory is that nothing's ever over. Every action you take is recorded permanently in the universe. I think if everybody understood that everything they do is permanent; maybe we'd all behave a little bit better because we'd want to make sure that those permanently recorded actions didn't reflect badly."

Astrophysicist Jeffrey Bennett Ph.D. to George Noory
on his program *Beyond Belief*

Photographs, snapshots and, to be concise, images of any kind hold several types of energy. They're actually containers housing an incredible amount of primary source information about us and our world. However, that *potential energy*[7] can't be freed from the confines of its two-dimensional package without the cooperation of at least one live human being. There are a number of factors which converge to support this speculation, and I will go into a few of them, but the expansion of conversation is the topic of another book.

In this short, how-to field guide I want to show you step-by-step techniques you can use to begin to "see" some shapes, patterns, and signs within the borders of a chosen image. I've written and rewritten this little book several times in order for it to be instructive. I want it to show you how to see the messages in your photos and snapshots in a simple, straightforward way without spending too much time exploring the more esoteric and scientific whys and hows.

First and foremost, I want you to discover that uncovering the messages in your images is a fabulously entertaining activity. Once you experience the process, then you'll be ready for all the explanations. Or not. Either way, you're about to embark on a new type of adventure.

Let's agree to just a few ground rules that will start you down the road of this fascinating process.

1. **You're a unique and singular entity upon the face of the earth.** No one remotely like you has ever lived before. Nobody has ever lived the life you've lived thus far. You— and the circumstances of your life—are a one-of-a-kind occurrence.

2. **Everything is composed of energy.** We experience energy in its countless forms all day, every day. We take it for granted that the electrical energy coming out of the wall sockets in our homes powers everything from our toaster to our computers. We don't think twice about pouring gasoline (liquid energy) into our car's tank, where the construction of the engine converts it to the force that enables it to run. Nor do we usually contemplate how emptying the contents of a big bowl of cereal or a banana (solid energy) into our stomachs is ultimately changed into the critical fuel that keeps all of the intricate mechanics of our bodies going from morning to night and, many times, for up to a century of life.

3. **When the shutter of the camera is clicked, a cascade of hundreds of processes are activated.** Both natural, elemental forces and human-created technologies meet in the "dark chamber" of the camera. The results are both mechanical and magical, spontaneous and enduring.

4. **The cosmos in which we exist is comprised of basic shapes, patterns and colors.** Throughout our collective time on the planet as humans, we've attached ancient meanings to what appear to us as elemental and primary forms and colors. Although different cultures may vary a bit on their connotations, throughout history each form has proven to be understood in similar ways by people all over the planet, no matter the distance separating them geographically.

5. **When you recognize the basic shapes, patterns and colors within an image, you'll take hold of a "key" that will enable you to "unlock" messages embedded in it when the impression was made.** Your focused attention in identifying an element within the borders of your image allows a deluge of information and stored energy to be released. Your awareness that the shape, color or pattern exists is the spark which unleashes the latent power of the picture.

6. **By understanding that you're both the seer and the interpreter of the sign, you'll decode a message embedded in the image mediated by the shape, pattern or color.** These fundamental forms communicate with our intuitive intelligence. That's the part of us that doesn't speak in words. Some call it "the right brain" of concepts and symbols as opposed to "the left brain" of reason and linearity. At this point, I'm not sure it matters very much how we explain it.

When we ride our bikes, we don't dissect which part of our brain is experiencing the enjoyment. When we swim, we don't analyze the various reasons we're having fun. Becoming adept at seeing the messages in your images is a new type of adventure, an expedition in visual awareness. It's no less exhilarating even though you're sitting in a chair and staring at your photographs. As I've said before, when you're ready for the science, I'll have some links on my website. I'll also be writing more about it on my website blog and in future books.

7. **The invention and incorporation of the camera into our evolution is more revolutionary to us than just simply as a mechanical device.** When we use an image recorder, which we know more intimately as a camera, it becomes an awesome instrument capable of producing the most amazing and enchanting intrigues.

Consider for a moment what a camera really does: it captures reality and transforms it into eternity.

The arcane chemistry practiced by ancient scientists known as "alchemists" claimed to transform a cheap metallic substance, like iron or tin, into another precious one such as gold. Precisely the same "alchemy" occurs between the subject and the photo–grapher (light-writer) at the instant of capture. The "ordinary" energy of a split-second is trapped and frozen in a virtual time capsule on the surface of film or into digital information. It's preserved—perhaps forever.

Strangely, the arrested power waiting there can only be activated when it's viewed by a real, living person. Its dynamic, stored information is "lifeless" without an observer to "turn on" its potential energy.

There's an undeniable relationship between people and their photos. It's a magnetic kinship that's ignited by our intention. The information that's been waiting— as if frozen in time—begins to thaw. We manually flip on the switch by deliberately examining an image that interests us. When we gaze with purpose, we activate a photo's inert energy. Suddenly something you've glimpsed many times in the past miraculously offers up something new. Something unexpected! You realize, as if by some magician's illusion, that the image looks back at you. It interacts with you through your attention to it.

8. The more you interact with your photographic images, the more energy you cause to be released. Suddenly, your intentional exploration of what's been confined between the borders (or on your computer screen) triggers a remarkable transformation: Your pictures will begin to open their secrets to you. They'll speak to you in the intuitive language you knew before all the culturally-learned words and numbers got caught in between and caused static in the reception.

What does the realization of this new information offer you? Some people experience insights into their "quirky" thoughts or behaviors. Others are able to connect seemingly disjointed incidences and people from their past in a way that evidences a larger, overall plan they've steadily, yet unwittingly, followed throughout their lives. People who are able to decode a few messages in their images discover that they are suppressing pre-verbal memories. When we're informed, as preschoolers or kindergartners, that the language we arrived with isn't valued in our impending education, we assume that our parents, grandparents and teachers are correct. We love them; we want to please them. So we make it a priority to forget our elemental communication system just as they did before us.

Everyone who focuses on their personal snapshots and photographs eventually reads his or her own messages in vastly different but incredibly intimate ways. No matter which type of experience you have, the most important aspect to remember is the awareness that occurs when you perceive yourself—maybe for the very first time—within the context of who you are, nestled inside of this particular present moment in history.

That one recognition will enable you to discover a focus in the present moment that will enhance your everyday life far into your future.

Chapter Note:

7. potential energy. (n.d.). The American Heritage® Stedman's Medical Dictionary. Retrieved October 08, 2014, from Dictionary.com website: http://dictionary.reference.com/browse/potential energy.

TIME IN A BOTTLE

"A picture shows me at a glance what it takes dozens of pages of a book to expound."
Russian writer Ivan Turgenev, *Fathers and Sons*, 1862

"Un bon croquis vaut mieux qu'un long discours."
("A good sketch is better than a long speech.")
Napoléon Bonaparte

A long time ago in the mid 1960s, when I started noticing the magic in my family's snapshots and photographs in magazines, there was no such thing as digital imaging. Television was a huge part of our lives at that time, probably more so than it is now.

Back then, I was seated in front of it at least a couple of hours every day along with my parents and my brother. I never missed a *Star Trek* episode or a *Man From Uncle* weekly installment. I think I must have already gotten some sort of impression from those futuristic shows that we were entering into a digital age, even though I had no idea what that might mean. When I walked into the Boeing Museum in Seattle, in about 1998, I was speechless when I pulled my cell phone out of my purse and compared it with the communicator prop from *Star Trek* they had on display in the glass case before me.

Left: *Star Trek's* Captain, James T. Kirk, (played by William Shatner) communicates with his starship Enterprise in a segment from around the year 1967. Right: A cell phone similar to mine from 1997.

I've discovered there were patents pending on camera/phone combinations that date back to as early as 1956, when I was two years old. That's incredibly interesting to me because it appears that, for the majority of my life, there have been engineers, designers and scientists diligently working to create a personal communicator camera. They were literally wishing, dreaming and willing it into existence.

I believe I felt their ideas were on their way.

I think we all did on some level—an unnamed excitement and innovation bubbling up from the imaginative depths of so many visionaries. Frequently an unspecific thrill ran through us, preparing us for an extraordinary shift in the very fabric of our civilization. It's hard to explain to people now. We were the ones (nicknamed the "Baby Boomers") who lived when every day seemed to get better than the last. It was probably because we watched television. We went to movies. We believed commercials. Certainly the photographs in *Life* and *Time* magazines exposed the horror of war and famine. Yet it didn't dampen the impression that a new and improved world was waiting for us.

It was a very special time. I, like anyone else who's ever landed on earth, had no control over where I touched down. I was lucky. Or not. I could only have the perspective of a little white girl born in the Southwestern part of the United States. I've felt guilty and I've also felt angry. The images that document my years here have helped me realize that I'm an historical character. The specific details of my life are the scaffold of my life story.

A great many people I've interviewed feel a strange time shift between the way the world was when they were children and the way it is today. We can literally sense the physical difference in the manner in which time passed 40 to 50 years ago. It was a much different place. Yet only a blink of an eye (perhaps less than a blink) in the span of history.

In spite of the allure of the television and movies, it was the still photographs that drew me in. They were the focus. They were the fascination.

I was in elementary school in the 60s when it truly was a black and white world. With many shades of gray as well. Almost all of the newspapers and magazines published non-color photos. It's interesting when I take the time to contemplate how being "exposed" to that form of imagery forged my ability to see shapes in a strikingly fundamental way. Combine that with the fact that there wasn't the overwhelming competition for my visual attention. As I write on my laptop, I'm casting my memories back to the class where I was learning to type on a manual typewriter. As I sink into a reverie, I still have some remnants of an image of myself in a remote cabin somewhere in the North woods, rhythmically tapping out my manuscripts on a vintage Royal or a tough and sea-salted Halda. And, naturally, those musings are accompanied by illusions of me, with my Leica camera, silently stalking the early morning animals as they slink out of their nests and burrows in the bluish mist. Or possibly I'm using my Hasselblad on that particular morning.

But when I'm totally honest with myself: I love my laptop sans the awfully, messy typewriter ribbons. I adore my Nikon DSLR and my iPhone, which don't require unbelievably stinky chemicals to render an image. It reminds me of when I interviewed my grandmother, born in 1903 on a farm in the Texas backwoods. I asked her if she missed anything about the lack of technology from the old days (like washing machines, autos, planes and refrigerators). She looked at me for about a half-a-minute and then slowly shook her head, "No. I can't say that I do."

Left: My paternal great-grandmother in 1899 in Trion, Georgia. Upper Right: My maternal grandmother in 1962 in Norman, Oklahoma. The bicycle "happened" to be in both photos.

I've thought about the transition from analog to digital for many years. My photography and writing have evolved right alongside everybody else's. When my husband and I were pursuing our degrees in the newly created Media Arts program at the University of South Carolina back in the 1970s, we were using actual film and running it through a 35mm camera body. There were about a hundred things that could go awry.

There was no automatic setting. We used light meters and, truth be known, crossed our fingers that we were getting the correct exposure and focus. Then, if we ever hoped to see what we'd captured, we'd have to go into a lightless room where we'd develop our film in the dark by blindly loading it onto a reel and pouring a solution we'd mixed up earlier into the container. We'd pour the developer out. Pour some fixer in, wash that out with another chemical. Then we'd hang our negatives to dry. We'd have to wait for a while, sometimes overnight, and concoct a whole different sort of chemistry to make the prints.

To be honest, there's actually nothing more exciting to a photographer in the moment than seeing an image you've been trying to coax from the ether slowly, and miraculously, appear on a sheet of wet paper in the tray under the glowing red lights of the darkroom.

That's how it used to be done. I imagine there are some diehard film folks who still love the craft so much they endure the whole process of making images with chemicals. For me, and for everybody else I know personally, we've been thrilled and sparked creatively by the innovations in digital imaging. I never really liked breathing in the fumes from the toxic chemicals or the burning of my skin when I processed and printed my negatives. There was no other way to go then. If you wanted your own photo, done your way, you had to get yourself to a darkroom and deal with it.

Today, when I think of dumping those caustic chemicals down the drain to filter into our planet's water system, it makes me feel sad that we were so unconnected to our tender environment. The other gift I believe digital imaging gives us is a cleaner world. Yet as a result of taking so many photographs on film, I have a great many negatives and their resulting pieces of printed paper.

Depending on when you began taking photos, you'll have a few different ways you can interact with your images.

You may also have inherited a lot of scrapbooks or boxes full of family photos.

And slides.

And disks.

It can be overwhelming.

My absolute favorite way to "read" one of my photos is to scan an image that I have on paper and transform it into a digital image. I discover so much more to look at when I can zoom in and really take my time examining it.

Next, we'll start delving into the process I use to gather and choose my own images (and to guide others in deciding on an image to examine), regardless of the form in which the image resides.

Just keep in mind though: We're only going to examine one single image this time. You may already have a picture selected.

That's just fine. After you step through the technique once, you can repeat it as many times as you wish.

THE SIGNS IN YOUR SNAPSHOTS

"The image itself will show you the way."

A line from the *Corpus Hermeticum*, wisdom texts from second and third centuries CE, translated by Marsilio Ficino in the 1400s

Look inside the boxes under the bed. Poke around inside the drawers that are seldom opened. Open up the unmatched photo albums spanning decades of time. Scroll through the files on the hard drive of the computer on your desk.

Somewhere, in one of those places, you'll find treasures.

Gems.

Riches.

The wealth hidden inside the masterpieces you find aren't the sort of assets you can hawk at an art auction for millions. Most likely, the value will only be recognized by you. Their bounties exist simply and purely for you. They endure for your edification. For your inspiration. For your illumination.

And really, isn't that enough?

You'll find them disguised as out-of-focus photos. Blurred snapshots. Dog-eared prints. Faded light impressions.

Up to this point in time, you may have only given them a brief glance. And, since you didn't intentionally devote the time to explore the information stored within their borders, you didn't notice the greater image nestled within the obvious one. Since you didn't engage, neither did the image.

I'm going to show you how to crack open the deeper, wider story that awaits you inside your personal photographs. You're headed for a great adventure.

Strangely enough, lots of images have been waiting for you to begin this journey since they were captured. Patiently pausing within their borders. You see, time has a very different nature when you're interacting with your images. Time slowed to a complete stop at the very instant the shutter clicked. It opened and closed.

That is the state in which it remains until you intentionally look at it. When you engage your full attention, you jumpstart the clock. Yet you're not only in the past and the present time, you're also in the "meantime." You've entered into the space of everything that occurred between the moment the image was captured and the moment when you interact with the image. You now know all that has happened in the time between those two points in your history. You've lived the "future" this picture preceded.

When you apply the techniques introduced here, you'll begin to understand that there's much more to the construction of your life than you perceived as you lived it in the moment. There's a conscious design to it. The people. The situations. The locations. The light. It's visible in your photographs. As you deeply absorb your images, it's almost as if you're in a low-flying plane, skimming over a village. You can easily see the town square. You can see the oval ponds and the rectangular houses. You can follow the horizontal fence lines. You can make out the thought processes and conscious decisions that arranged the whole metropolis in the way it's laid out.

I realize that this may sound fantastic, but once you witness it, your perception will shift. For centuries, gifted artists have been concealing symbols and signs in plain sight within their paintings. *The Da Vinci Code* was a worldwide bestseller because readers (and later movie audiences) are acutely aware that all sorts of clues are embedded in classical art and architecture. Those who can actually decipher the messages inserted by the medium of paint often wonder how the play of light and shadow, the application of colors and shapes, is able to morph into timeless sorts of communications. Did the painter plant them on purpose or are they the appearance of meaningful design "accidents"?

Here's an even more intriguing question: Does the interaction of light, color, shadow, tone and perspective on a two-dimensional surface create the perfect environment for the field of all possibilities (Spirit, Life, the Creator, Nature) to express itself for the sake of communication from wherever it dwells to our perceptions within a three-dimensional reality? Consider the premise offered by the

Greek mathematician and philosopher Plato, sometime around the fourth century BC: "Perhaps there is a pattern set up in the heavens for one who desires to see it, and having seen it, to find it in himself." Or herself. Thank you very much, Mr. Plato.

I've been able to see the worlds within images since I was a child. After I realized that other people didn't perceive images as I did, I kept my natural ability to myself for a really long time. Yet there came a moment, about three years ago, when I became convinced that sharing my perspective was, more than likely, simply a step in the evolutionary process of photography. That there were probably many other people who might be able to see the messages evident in photographs (particularly snapshots) if it were introduced to them. I have found that supposition to be correct as I've traveled around and shown my techniques to folks who are interested.

So this is a primer. It's an introduction to demonstrate the methods I use to see the patterns, signs, symbols and messages in my own and other people's personal images. If you try even a couple of the techniques, I can guarantee it will amaze you and you'll never regard your (or anyone else's) photographs in the same way again. The ability to see and know, in this case with your snapshots, requires nothing of you but a willingness to open your mind to the possibility that our "reality" is an interactive, dynamic place. You'll have to gently nudge yourself into the mindset that, as humans, we filter out of our consciousness what we can't easily process.

Many times we only perceive the shadows or the first layer of people, places, and things that are, in fact, multi-dimensional. Our awareness only scratches the surface of the infinite wonder that lies beyond and beneath our capacity of understanding. We have the ability to change that limitation though.

Ultimately the greatest gift delivered by the process of what I call "image alchemy" is that it helps us to perceive the miraculous and magical phenomena that are ever present in our daily lives. Once you witness how the signs and communications have been documented in your photographs, you'll realize that wonder-filled moments are happening at breathtaking, breakneck speeds in every instant of every day.

The camera is an instrument

*that teaches
people to see*

WITHOUT A CAMERA

*dorothea
lange*

A FEW THINGS TO CONSIDER... ABOUT LIFE ON EARTH, LIGHT AND CAMERAS, YOUR JOURNEY TO THIS PLANET, AND MISSION CONTROL

"Intuition becomes increasingly valuable in the new information society precisely because there is so much data."

John Naisbitt, Author of *Megatrends*

The universe (Cosmos, Spirit, Life-force) wants to talk to you. Well, that's not quite accurate. It's already talking to you. It's been communicating with you for all of eternity. If that's too much for you to accept, then at least for the amount of time you've been present on this planet. There are all sorts of types of communication.

Don't believe me?

Then just try holding your breath for a minute or so. Even if you want to stop breathing, you just can't do it! Your body is in intimate contact with of the whole of life and life will prevail. You'll breathe because everything in your physiology hears the signal to breathe. Something demands that it keep going. Inside your incredibly well-equipped life-suit vehicle, everything is wired in place for you to navigate on this beautiful blue planet you're visiting.

Let's take that idea a little farther before we go on.

Imagine you're an extraterrestrial voyager to Earth who landed (coincidentally) on your birthday and (synchronistically) in your birth year. Back at Mission Control (wherever that is; I can't remember, can you?) there are those who have a profound interest in helping you complete the purpose for which you were dispatched. That you're drawn to very specific types of interest here on Earth is evidence you're on an important assignment. At times it feels as if you're driven to pursue something in particular. Those pastimes, pursuits, hobbies, passions, recreations and avocations are on purpose. You were designed to recognize those as signs because they're leading you to toward accomplishing your mission.

Hospice workers and those who attend the dying report that the most frequent regret among people in the process of passing on is they realize their heartbreak over not pursuing their own "dream."[8] They wished they'd lived a life that aligned with their awareness of their true selves instead of being pushed into the duties demanded by others. "Dream" is simply another word for mission, assignment, task or calling. It's interesting we call it our "dream," as if it's a fantasy that came out of our own heads instead of being an integral part of our reason for being alive.

Now back to the way photographs (especially snapshots) relate to the visitor-from-another-planet scenario.

How would those observing us from Mission Control try to communicate with us? We don't carry any concrete recollections about our shared language. It seems that one of the conditions we had to agree upon before we were launched, as it were, was we were bound to touch down here (encased in our baby human-suits) with fresh minds. It was of the utmost importance that we be freed from proclivities or preconceptions about our place of origin in order to be fully and completely Earthlings. We had to be ready to take on the peculiarities that are resident to this unique planet.

So we arrived as a newborn: helpless and teachable.

For about four or five years, we teetered between two worlds: the one from which we'd come and the one into which we'd landed. We learned the language of the culture into which we were born but we were also allowed to retain (just for those first formative years) a symbolic language from our original home. We literally based our understanding of our new cultural environment from our recognition of shapes, forms, patterns and colors. Of course, smells, tastes and temperature had an influence as well. They grounded us here and introduced the physical sensations present on the earth.

As soon as we could get our tiny little hands on a writing implement, we drew circles and lines and squares. We would run to our parents or caregivers, our small faces beaming with satisfaction. The grownups (who had forgotten these ancient and universal symbols) would smile sweetly as they glanced at our "primitive" scribbling, thinking we were simply doing what all toddlers do. We were making feeble attempts to scratch out some semblance of the same reality they saw.

They couldn't have been more wrong.

That's not what we were doing at all. We were trying to show the "big" people that there's a shared code in the cosmos. We recalled just that much. We didn't know exactly what it meant but we knew it meant something important.

"See, Mom! I remembered!" That's the message we were wanting to communicate. Yet, all we little spirits encased in human suits are hobbled with the same limitations. We don't recall exactly who "they" might be. And the older we get, the less bold the outlines become. But, when we're young, we recognize the signs when we see them.

There are countless religious traditions from all over the planet that have built temples to "them" even though they can't agree who "they" are either. Throughout our entire lives, we are tapped on the shoulder by the universal signs, symbols, and patterns. Just as our distant ancestors were before us. They tried their best to communicate it forward to us by scratching the messages they received upon their cave walls and cliffs.

Yes, that's the way Mission Control sends us signals. It's how the Universe, the Great Spirit, God, Prana, Life, Fate, The Field of All Possibilities (choose whatever word works best for you) broadcasts. At least that's one of the important vehicles of communication. Visual artists are the sector of our population who seem to sense this contact intuitively. It's exactly the force inspiring them to find a subject to commit to paper or canvas or photograph or film. Often, they'll tell you they don't exactly understand why they want to explore something. They simply know they must do it or they'll feel unfulfilled. When they go ahead and follow their artistic instincts, they see and know a fragment of an essential concept they were compelled to understand.

Here's how the world-renowned painter, Georgia O'Keeffe, explained the obsession that prompted her to create her art: "I found I could say things with colors and shapes that I couldn't say any other way—things I had no words for."

In her biography, O'Keeffe recalls her first recollection of lying beside her mother on a spring or summer day in 1888 in Sun Prairie, Wisconsin. She supposes she was about six months old. "My first memory is of the brightness of light...light all around. I was sitting among pillows on a quilt on the ground...very large white pillows…"

From that single memory she carried with her all of her entire 99 years of life, she knew she was meant to be an artist. It was her mission. Her assignment. Her burden and her strength. She made it her job to maintain the memory of the shapes and the forms. But mostly, she remembered the light. A particular quality of light that deeply affected her for just short of a century on Earth and produced some of the most profoundly impactful images ever created by a visual artist.

Symbols, shapes, patterns, light, dark and colors are the elements that comprise the vocabulary of our shared first language, regardless of where we landed upon the face of the planet. When we're born, we all possess a common form of reception even though we have no way to communicate it. Our bodies haven't yet acquired the steadiness or the ability to relay it to anyone else. We simply appear as babies to the people with whom we come into contact. When, in fact, we're oh so much more.

Light and cameras interact together like spirit and humans do. Invisible, intangible essences are rendered physically visible by its interplay with a mechanical counterpart. The evidence of this exchange is in the pictures produced as negatives, photographic prints, and digital image files. We have billions of "offspring" as proof of this spectacular cooperation by the seen and unseen.

Between the pages of your scrapbooks, among the data on your hard drive, and behind the glass of the wooden frame hanging in your hall are the unique testaments, the physical manifestations, that document your singular journey on Earth. They are essential keys for you to use to examine and unlock a deeper understanding of who you are, when you are and where you are.

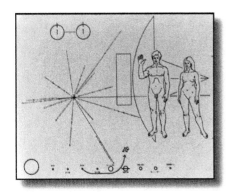 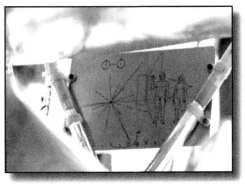

On the left: The "Pioneer Plaques," consisting of two gold-anodized aluminum plaques, were placed aboard the Pioneer 10 in 1972 and the Pioneer 11 spacecrafts in 1973 by NASA before they were launched. They are comprised of symbols that would convey information about earth should it ever be intercepted by extraterrestrial beings.

On the Right: The first "Pioneer Plaque" attached to the Pioneer 10 spacecraft when it was launched in 1972. Images courtesy of Wikipedia.

Chapter Note:

8. Martino, J. (2013, August 3). *The Top 5 Regrets of the Dying*. www.huffingtonpost.com. Retrieved October 8, 2014 from http://www.huffingtonpost.com/2013/08/03/top-5-regrets-of-the-dying_n_3640593.html.

PART TWO: SNAPSHOT ARCHEOLOGY

"...as my eyes grew accustomed to the light, details of the room within emerged slowly from the mist, strange animals, statues, and gold—everywhere the glint of gold. For the moment—an eternity it must have seemed to the others standing by—I was struck dumb with amazement, and when Lord Carnarvon, unable to stand the suspense any longer, inquired anxiously, 'Can you see anything?' it was all I could do to get out the words, 'Yes, wonderful things.'"

Howard Carter, upon entering the tomb of Tutankhamun

Every archeological dig begins with an historical site upon which some event occurred. Members of previous lifetimes may have left artifacts in the ground for researchers to unearth. We're very familiar with expeditions such as the excavation of King Tut's tomb in Egypt in 1922 by Howard Carter and George Herbert. The quote above are the words Carter used to describe the awe that overwhelmed him as he began to see ancient treasures hidden in the tomb for more than 30 centuries.

Not every archeological expedition is as grand or has as much international press coverage as the discovery of King Tut's tomb. Many are quiet undertakings led by archeologists or anthropologists who depend on the efforts of community volunteers to help them recover shards of pottery, belt buckles, pipe stems and other utensils from the past. Together they attempt to piece together an understanding of the people who inhabited that plot of ground and how they lived when they were alive. The excavated artifacts contain potential energy, albeit a slow-vibrating type, that conveys information about the individuals residing there from a previous point on our historical timeline

When you choose a photograph, or more specifically in this case a snapshot, from a specific time in your life, it's going to originate from a point earlier in your historical timeline. Because everything that happens after now...and now... and now....is the past. We're all moving. Always. Every fraction of a moment is discrete. We were there just an instant ago and now we're here.

And here.

Perhaps you can start to understand the importance of snapshots when you pause a while to consider the speeding trajectory of your everyday life. If this sounds like it's going to be an overwhelming idea to contemplate, don't be concerned. The first thing we're going to do to guide us into the dark and jumbled areas between the border of your snapshots is to find one, single shape.

You don't even need to physically hold an image in front of you in the form of a print on paper or see a digital image on your screen of choice (cell phone, tablet, laptop or desktop). Simply think about an element of a particular photo. All you need to do is close your eyes and consider the outline of a human body.

Can you find a basic shape in it?

Yes, of course you can.

You can look at a photo of a person in virtually any magazine or advertisement whose likeness is captured there. If the individual is looking toward the camera, you'll quickly realize the basic shape of his or her head is an oval. An oval is one of the most basic shapes in our world.

What's the first physical object that comes to your mind with the shape of an oval? Most likely it's that of an egg. The next question we ask ourselves is, "What does an egg represent?"

Food.

Breakfast.

Holidays.

Those are various meanings associated with an egg in several cultures throughout the world. But, what else might an egg symbolize?

In the ancient Persian Empire, eggs represented fertility, prosperity, rebirth and the return of spring. In one Eastern culture's wedding ceremony, an egg is passed over the groom's head in a circular motion and then cracked open to keep evil away from his new marriage. An egg is included in the Jewish Seder rites in celebration, and remembrance, of the freedom from slavery endured by the Hebrew people for over two centuries in Egypt.

Now consider, once again, the drawings of children. Their artwork offers incredible insight into the way we first interacted with basic shapes. Those primal, and very personal interpretations, are still residing in our subconscious. And perhaps not even that far under the surface. It doesn't take a great deal of stimulus to awaken those pre-verbal, childhood associations and draw them into our conscious perception.

This book is an introduction to a technique I've named "Snapshot Archeology" because I use that analogy as a way to explain a specific procedure you'll utilize to unearth the "artifacts" beneath the "topsoil" of your photographs. I'll show you how to use some methods I've developed to dig down into the images that fascinate or haunt you in some inexplicable way.

Whether you actually clicked the shutter yourself or somebody else performed the act, there's an undeniable magnetic quality to the images that document your life.

As a filmmaker of historical documentaries, I've spent a fair amount of time interviewing and observing archeologists and anthropologists as they investigate a site. The difference between anthropologists and archeologists is a very small one in the United States. The two are generally lumped into one category. However, in Europe, as well as in many other countries, anthropologists study the culture of a people and archeologists study the things people leave behind from their culture. They search for remnants of pottery, manuscripts, roads, tools and generally anything that may have survived weather and erosion.

One documentary I produced several years ago, that was beautifully filmed and directed by my husband, was an extensive expedition where no less than ten researchers dug, sifted, sorted and cataloged for six days each week. For six full weeks!

They toiled for ten hours a day during the months of June and July in South Carolina's 100-degree-plus heat with 60 percent humidity. The resulting 15-minute documentary, called *Pottersville*, follows the excavation of an alkaline glazed stoneware kiln that operated in the first half of the 19th century. The excavation conditions were brutal, but the mystery and the potential secrets the project held within the earth was just too full of mystery to the participants for them to allow little things like sun stroke and dehydration stop them.

Dr. George Calfas, of the University of Illinois at Urbana-Champaign, and his research assistants eventually unearthed the largest industrial slave-operated kiln ever found. Their back-breaking work somewhat gave a voice to the more than 13,000 enslaved Africans in the Edgefield, South Carolina, District, who worked the same long, sweltering hours to produce weighty storage vessels for pork, beans, okra and other staples essential to plantation life in the days before refrigeration. Except, of course, the enslaved people toiled—uncompensated—in the factory for more than a half century.

When the documentary was finally posted to our website (KoelkerAssociates. com), it was clear that the team's discoveries were of interest to other archeologists and historians throughout the world. Weekly field updates were posted to our company's video channel on the Web. Almost immediately, thousands of viewers from across the globe found them—a viral event occurred about this tiny, obscure world of industrial archeology.

To me, it was yet another testament to the power of the secrets in the artifacts that are patiently lying beneath the surface of something. Waiting to be seen. Waiting to be heard.

Finally, it was proven that the design of the kiln was fashioned after a Chinese version that was thousands of years old. No one had any idea that it would turn out to be the largest kiln of its type in the United States—and, for that matter, in most of the world—until they started to dig. Until they started to upturn a vast area of broken pieces of pottery. Charred bricks. Worn tools.

The things that were left behind for later.

It was a surprise.

It was magic.

Your photographs, particularly your snapshots, document what you've left behind. They document who you were within a certain context at a particular period in historical time. Snapshots and photographs are where we start today when we want to follow where we've been. Personally, I believe the major reason photography has evolved into the integral aspect of our daily (almost momentary) lives that it's become is we've longed to investigate where we've been. To take another look back at that road we ran down so quickly. We're not allotted nearly enough years to deduce where we fit into the scheme of things. And, as we go forward in our transformational evolution on the planet, we want to see for ourselves that our lives counted for something, that we were part of the whole picture.

This is an extraordinary period of time for our personal involvement in the transformation of our home planet. In many ways we're not much different than the other explorers who've been curious about lands far away from their own throughout human history. Although we haven't been to the deepest parts of the ocean yet, we've managed to traverse almost the entire surface of the earth. In a strangely similar way, we're exploring our life here in this visual place in space gripping our cameras instead of the rails of a Spanish galleon: probing beyond the limits of imagination with technology that hadn't even been manifested in the physical world until the 1820s.

With the contributions of notable psychic coaches and psychologists—ranging from Carl Jung to Wayne Dyer and Marianne Williamson—who have helped us understand our importance in the evolution of humankind; we've finally given ourselves permission to trust our intuition with regard to the body and mind housing our spirits. Up until a very few years ago, we relied on other people to help us "know" ourselves. We were programmed to be nervous about looking at our interior landscape as it appears in the headlights of the big, wide universe. With the advent of the Internet and our ability to fact check our "crazy" ideas, our minds and psyches have been freed to experience the literally billions of ways we perceive life (the Cosmos, the Creator....you get the idea). We can peruse the sites and blogs we encounter to decide for ourselves if our individual perceptions are outliers or are only firmly pushing against the walls of the box in which we've been banging around for centuries. We must do everything we can to keep the Internet an open source for expression; it's the dawning of a truly democratic platform.

However, in the midst of the freedom we must keep learning how to trust what we see about ourselves without the undue influence of advertisements or billboards, gurus or media preachers, swamis or salesman. We must craft our own paths forward from the artifacts we identify around us: physically, spiritually and virtually. We must utilize those shards of observation left for us by others who went before. Those without the benefit (or hindrance) of an ever-present media.

In other words, I'm not only suggesting you embrace the visually overwhelming images produced by the media but that you also become adept at choosing the images you intuit will serve your own journey. We're fully empowered to pick up the pieces we find and slide them into our lives, or not. We can use them to fit the puzzle together to make a complete—or at least a more complex picture—of ourselves within the period of historical time in which we exist.

Or we can leave them where they lie.

In either case, we're able to discern what we're seeing.

We initiate this process of seeing and knowing by digging into our snapshots.

The National Science Foundation classifies archeology as a social science. Many times, in universities, it's taught under their humanities programs. The important concepts in plain sight here are: social, science and human. To be social means to live in interaction with other people. It denotes living in a community. It infers having a life involved with other human beings. Science, of course, means a systematic study of the way things work in the natural, physical world, primarily by using experiments and observations.

For many of us, science has taken on a few aspects of spirituality that the regimented religious systems were unable to represent into, as some would categorize it, their corporate structure. A lot of us have learned to trust science, with its delineated rules and repeatable results, a great deal more then we trust the religions to which we were first exposed.

I've heard a number of physicists, biologists and other scientists comment that they were led down the path of rigorous experimentation and observation as a result of being born into war-torn countries where conflicting ideologies and religious dogmas were dispensed, often out the business end of a gun. They felt they couldn't make a heartfelt decision based on any "truths" they experienced on the opinions of people in their lives. They couldn't discern who was right and who was not by simply observing their words and actions. They needed a more rigorous structure within which to operate. So they became scientists.

Snapshot Archeology came about for me as a result of my working closely with and observing archeologists. I connected with the structure in which they work. There's a precise way they began each of their forays into a location that might hold some secrets worth exploring. They're scanning. They're searching. They're on the look out for particular signs, patterns and circumstances when they're considering a potential dig site.

I was once led around a large field adjacent to an old plantation house in South Carolina while two archeologists explained to me that the various bumps and raised areas on the surface of the land I was stumbling over were probably either foundations of cabins or garbage heaps from at least a century and a half ago. Those particular spots held a great deal of information about the people who lived upon that piece of land. To me they just appeared as a slightly elevated mounds of dirt. And really not even that much of a difference in height as the rest of the acreage around it. However, to the trained eye of the archeologist, it was a possible excavation spot that might yield treasures, in the form of artifacts, about the people who had existed there a long time ago.

That's exactly the way I always scanned my own personal snapshots. Instead of walking through a field, I would visually step across the surface of an image. And although I can also see the signals in other people's images, my own were always much more magnetic for me. Some small aspect of the picture would draw my attention to it. The problem for me was that I didn't really understand what I was observing until I devised a technique for advancing through a process that gave a structure to what I was experiencing. I knew I gained new information from a two-dimensional surface of a photograph but I didn't connect the "geography" of it to the archeology of it.

Although I wouldn't say geography was my best subject in school, it's also an integral part of this process. Geography, topography, cartography (map making) and archeology. An abbreviated and specialized structure of each of them comes into play when you get serious about actually seeing what's waiting for you in your snapshots.

It helps me to use analogies when I refer to what occurs when I look at an image. One of them is that of an archeologist, as I've just explained. My mind follows my eyes to a point of interest where I see something that intrigues me. Something that I imagine will yield an insight of one kind or another. Something that will bring to me a bit of information that interests or serves me.

Another frequent analogy I use is that of standing on the bank of a relatively clear pool of water. As I gaze over the edge of the pool (while I'm really looking at an image either on paper or on a computer screen) I can see that there are ripples stirring up the clarity of the pond water. In other words, my perception of the surface of the image I'm looking at is not yet focused. Yet underneath, and down at the bottom of the light, sandy floor of the pool (sometimes a darker, muddy substance) I see the outlines of a shape. I can make out a crude form.

Immediately, I know that's the area I want to go first. So I dive off into the pool, still in the analogy, with my arms extended in front of me. I swim straight for the shape or the form I saw while standing on the bank. When I reach the shape, I know that I can either stay put and look around from that vantage point or I can paddle off in another direction.

I might discover some other shape, color or pattern that interests me from my position beneath the water. I can decide to swim over to explore another area, with the knowledge that I can always return to my home base at any time. That's the way I keep my orientation within the photograph/pool.

Both of the analogies serve me well. They also help other people understand that, even though their physical bodies are not moving around inside the photograph per se, their eyes are "swimming" in the image. They are naturally the physical organs that allow us to do the actual finding and following of a shape.

It can be disorienting to "dive down" into an image. It's easy to lose your way because forms change once you're inside. Some shapes get bigger. Some angles seem to shift. You can begin to examine one aspect so closely that you lose the perspective you had when you began the "dive." There are lots of clues to follow and also lots of dead ends. But that's the same journey you take when you're involved in pursuing any expedition, mystery or quest.

The high of the adventure is to approach your photos and snapshots as the rich and wonderful historical sites that they are. When you dive into the experience with that attitude, you can't be disappointed.

"Always remember that you are absolutely unique. Just like everybody else."

Margaret Mead, cultural anthropologist, 1901–1978

A SNAPSHOT IS DIFFERENT
FROM ALL OTHER TYPES OF IMAGES

"A good snapshot stops a moment from running away."
Eudora Welty, 20th century Southern author and photographer

Snapshots Are the Holy Grail of Images

A "grail" is a cup or a vessel. It's most often used in conjunction with a mystical and, probably, mythical cup from which Jesus Christ drank at the Last Supper. The Knights of King Arthur's Round Table searched for it. The Knights Templar protected it. In the story told by a movie, Indiana Jones and his father were nearly killed for it.

A snapshot is also a vessel. It contains elements which may be considered "holy" or "pure," insofar as they're held inside an image in an uncorrupted type of frozen form of stillness. Considering that thousands or millions (perhaps billions) of happenstances had to take place, exactly as they occurred, for a specific personal image to exist in its present form is literally mind-boggling.

Remember that a snapshot is always a photograph but a photograph is not always a snapshot.

For an image to be placed in the category of a snapshot, it must have been originally captured within at least one of these situations:

1. An informal, casual image

2. An image that was captured quickly

3. An image in which artistic intent was not the main reason for its creation

4. An image that has only minimal arrangement of subject matter

5. Generally, an image that was handheld (no tripod)

6. An image taken by an amateur (although "professionals" can create snapshots under the conditions stated here)

7. An image of an occurrence that happened briefly or only a single time

8. An image which has not been manipulated by an image editing software

9. An uncropped image

Nobody is looking over your shoulder to correct you if you want to investigate a particular image that interests you. However, the spontaneous nature of an image captured in one of the above situations naturally holds more energy, together with a synchronistic aspect, that you'll come to anticipate and appreciate. It will give you a specific sort of thrill when you start to see facets of a snapshot opening up to your gaze. You'll soon recognize that there are factors at play in snapshots that simply aren't explainable in words. It has to be seen to be believed.

Did you ever wonder why other people's stories" seem so much more compelling than your own? As I've learned, through applying what I've come to term "image alchemy," it's all about our individual perspectives. More precisely put, it's where we are mentally in our point of observation. When you practice shifting your attention from somebody else's viewpoint about life or history or movies to the sweeping and visually panoramic scenes from your own astonishing story, I can pretty much guarantee that you'll experience the world, and particularly yourself, in an entirely altered way.

It's a shift that bestows upon you a definite wonder about the remarkable entity you are. It's not an absorption with yourself in a narcissistic or neurotic way. It's an appreciation of yourself as unique in all the universe. A conscious testament to acknowledge your brief walk through this world as valuable. This awareness assures that you'll also value everyone else as a sensational, singular character as well. You'll love more and you'll live more fully. You just can't help yourself.

A big promise I realize, but true nonetheless.

So let's get started because the more you know about the power of an image, the more dominion you'll begin to feel in your everyday life. And the more of that kind of control you feel, the higher you'll want to fly. And the more altitude you gain, the more you'll see your whole cosmos from an interconnected and balanced frame of reference. You'll quite literally see your life through a different lens.

When Is a Photograph More Than Just a Piece of Paper?

While I was in the beginning process of writing this book in early 2014, the International Center of Photography in New York was hosting an exhibition of 84 works by 21 contemporary photo artists which, in the words of the curator Carol Squiers, "explores the range of creative experimentation that has occurred in photography since the 1970s."[10] The title of the exhibition (and an accompanying book) was a question: *What Is a Photograph?*

I began working in the world of commercial photography and image making in the early 70s. I can relate to the relevance of asking the question, "what is a photograph?" I've spent way too many hours (probably years if I totaled all the time up!) behind a carefully locked door in a darkroom. The entire time I was closed up in that tiny, black closet of a place, I was either mixing chemicals or pouring chemicals. Worst of all, I was breathing chemicals and allowing them to seep into my skin. But those were just a few of the attentive measures that all serious photographers had to endure if they wanted to have control over their images. They hoped that if they religiously followed the protocol for developing and printing, they'd eventually behold the images they'd mindfully captured on their precious film emulsion.

Those were apprehensive stretches of time, when one mistake in either the processing solution or the developing mixture could demolish our picture and kill the prospect for a masterpiece. At least for that go-round. We were certain, no doubts whatsoever, that we'd captured magic on our exposed film. We were sure of it! It compelled us to stand in the dark and allow ourselves to be exposed to all manner of toxicities. We were duty bound to go through the precise alchemical process of coaxing the reluctant image to show itself.

And oh how much time and money and effort and sweat and hopes we invested in that undertaking! It was our visual art after all. Artists will go to any lengths to bring the reality of their inner vision into the light. There was no doubt in our minds that we were artists. Even if we were just getting paid to do a little photo shoot for a mom-and-pop business in our little town, the perfection of the image was all that mattered. We wouldn't have allowed anyone to refer to our photographic images as snapshots. It was a sacrilege we would never have accepted.

On the other hand, when we'd take quick shots of our friends and family—that we prayed to goodness none of our other professional/commercial/artist photographer cohorts ever laid their perfectly composed eyes on—we'd proceed just like all the other non-professionals who had a roll of film to develop. We'd head over to the cheapest photo boutique at the closest strip shopping center and let them do all the work. We'd wait with veiled optimism while our non-composed, shot-on-the-run pictures went through the bourgeois procedures, bathing and bubbling in a wash of pre-measured chemicals over which we had no command.

Ultimately the day would come when we'd excitedly rush over to pick up our precious, yet obviously flawed, packet of prints. We'd happily and hurriedly hand over our money to the photo boutique clerk so we could hungrily tear into our treasure right there in front of God and everybody. And we'd completely accept that, even though they generally would never be "good enough" to ever have a snowball's chance in Hades of hanging in a frame on a wall in our home, these pieces of paper were golden. They were priceless. They were the images we would go back to over and over again. They were especially important because they were images documenting us in the midst of our real lives. They were "snapped" with an unguarded acceptance of the someone or something that synchronistically appeared before our camera lens. Yes, they were blurred and, yes, we'd wish something hadn't obscured some part of it accidentally. But mostly, they were perfectly, mystically, incredibly complete. There was a magic to them we couldn't verbalize.

Back to the exhibition I mentioned earlier in this chapter at the International Center of Photography, *What Is a Photograph?* Ken Johnson, a writer for the

New York Times, concluded, "The show doesn't answer the question. Rather it brings together works from the past four decades by 21 artists who have used photography to ponder photography, leaving [exhibition] viewers to figure it out for themselves."[11]

So the final answer, to all of us would-be photo artists, might be explained using a fragment of an adage. A photograph is "in the eye of the beholder." It's many things. It's art. It's drama. It's reality. It's sentimentality. It's documentary. But primarily, the meaning of a photograph conforms to how our eye(s), our GUT Gauge (more about that later) and our unconscious (subconscious, soul, spirit) interact with it. That's my definition, by the way, and the definition we'll use as a guidepost throughout our exploration of Snapshot Archeology.

Even though I always recognized the beauty and the amazing potential of personal snapshots as powerful documents of each person's physical body intersecting with a specific block of historical time, my "classical" training in the photo styles of the masters (Ansel Adams, Edward Weston, Yousuf Karsh) put the kibosh on my ever suggesting it as a respected form of study.

Well, I'll admit, I did bring it up once. It was ugly. My push for a legitimizing a more "off the cuff" type of image were met with smirks and snuffs. I don't blame those "professionals" anymore. I was right there, ultimately agreeing with their guidelines for artful and effective photography. To my credit, I was always hoping to slip my quiet observations in somewhere as the years passed. I continued to see messages in my snapshots as well as in those of other people, but I just decided to keep my comments to myself. Nobody else seemed to be talking about it or, for that matter, seeing it. Maybe I was imagining things that weren't there.

Also, over a 20 year period, I married two commercial photographers. I've since discovered this part of my attempt to squelch my intuition while continuing to hand over an authority to the old school notion of valid image making. Both men are incredibly talented craftspersons whom I very much admire and respect. And in a very real sense, their expertise has provided the contrast I needed to differentiate between a photograph and a snapshot.

There's a Zen proverb that always comes to mind when I get to this part of my story. It goes something like this: "Let go or be dragged." That line pretty much describes what eventually occurred in my life. I finally was forced to make peace with the reality that I'd allowed my personal vision to be invalidated by the old guys from the middle of the last century who'd made up rules about what a "good" photograph should be. It's not that I disagree with them. It's just that there's more than one way to look at an image. Photography critics spend endless hours scrutinizing what is and what isn't a "good" photo.

I eventually had to personally let go of all the dogma. It was hard for me to do. It was difficult to validate my personal vision and experience. Yet when I finally got out of the way, I discovered that my images had waited for me. When I let the mission lead, the rest was easy.

At some point around the early 2000s, I couldn't ignore the incredible attraction that "vernacular" snapshots had on me. Yes, I learned that certain images have an official name. Plenty of collectors are on the lookout for specific kinds of images made by amateurs (or even by those who've created uniquely everyday-looking images though they practice photography as a profession). There's also another sub-genre called "found photography." It categorizes old photos that have been abandoned or thrown out, for whatever reason, only to show up later at flea markets or in trash cans.

Examples of vernacular photographs are family celebration snapshots, old class portraits, photo booth images, vacation photos and ID pics. People who long ago cast aside their "mortal coil" are endlessly fascinating when their past likeness is viewed in a yellowed, dog-eared print, despite the foggy separation of past and present.

Are you noticing something intriguing right about now? Apparently, it seems that at this time in history we've begun to agree that all sorts of photographs contain some incredibly engaging data.

What's so special about this magic of capturing a representation of someone or something in a black box or a camera phone or a tablet?

It's also about the light.

Figuratively.

Metaphorically.

Scientifically.

Chapter Notes:

10. Squiers, C. (2014). *What is a Photograph?* Great Britain. Prestel Publishing, Random House.

11. Johnson, K. (2014, January 31). *Digital, Analog and Waterlogged*: 'What Is a Photograph?' Opens at the I.C.P. The New York Times, pp. C27.

LIGHTING OUR WAY INTO OUR SNAPSHOTS

"In the beginning God created the heavens and the earth. The earth was without form and void; and darkness was on the face of the deep. And the Spirit of God was hovering over the face of the waters. Then God said, 'Let there be light', and there was light. And God saw the light, that it was good, and God divided the light from the darkness."

The Judeo-Christian Bible, *Genesis* 1:1–4

Light is a big subject. Perhaps one of the biggest. Suffice it to say that we don't get very far without it.

We're going to get comfortable with a few concepts about light before we go any further. I'll keep it simple and streamlined because one of the brick walls that separates us from the messages in our images is the idea that someone must be a bone fide professional, certified to make assessments of images. Let's agree that if you have a phone and if it records images, you're a bone fide professional.

We all are.

Primarily, physical light refers to the portion of the electromagnetic radiation spectrum that can be seen by the human eye. The physical property of light is ambiguous. It is both a particle and a wave. This is known as the wave-particle duality of light. The important part of this as it relates to our interest in light and photos is that, when an observer is present to see the light, light changes its behavior from when there's nobody present and looking at it.

That is a critical point to remember as we're present and looking with intention at our images. Don't feel bad if you can't rationally understand it. Even Dr. Albert Einstein couldn't figure it out himself. He noted: "It seems as though we must use sometimes the one theory and sometimes the other, while at times we may use either. We are faced with a new kind of difficulty. We have two contradictory pictures of reality; separately neither of them fully explains the phenomena of light, but together they do."

Science has proved that light has an intelligence, albeit one that most of us have difficulty understanding. Yet, in some very basic way, we appreciate that this light possesses intelligence. This brilliance, if you will, is obvious. It has personality. It has expression. It has moods. It has preferences. It may play with you or it may dominate you. It chooses who and what it wants to be seen as. Even its name can change its manifestation. Though we call it sunlight, moonlight, starlight; it's really all the same light.

The most compelling part of it for me is the fact that in its physical structure light exists in two distinct forms. The wave is continuous and the particle is non-continuous. And, in quantum mechanics,[12] light also "decides" which form it will take as it is observed by us. I'm proposing that the light, which has been captured in an image, responds to our observing it. We, as the observers, are the key that unlocks the phenomenon which releases the "messages" in our images.

The Inner Light

Metaphorical light refers to the qualities of understanding, comprehension, beauty, insight and spiritual illumination.

No light = No sight.

Both physically and metaphorically.

Spiritually and bodily.

In most of our cultures' sacred stories we're told that before there was anything else, there was darkness. Then, into that seemingly endless void, into that solitary emptiness, came an element critical to humans and to all the life on our planet.

Light.

Illumination.

Radiance.

Luminescence.

The fundamental opposite of dark.

Without which there can be no sight.

Yet without the absence of light (the dark) there's no differentiation of anything at all. Only blackness. Or what we perceive as black is simply no light.

While we're at it, let's ponder some of the other individual characteristics of light. Think about the ways in which its various personas leap back and forth between what philosophers, theologians, physicists, and poets have been attempting to eternally quantify.

The physical presence of light allows us to see in our environment. The presence, or entrance of light in a metaphorical sense, allows us to "see" what we mean or what we mean to say.

"To see the light," when used as a figure of speech, explains our ability to call a perception we have in our mind out into a place where we can examine it.

Here are a few ways that notable people have referred to light:

"You are the light of the world." **Matthew 5:14**
   Quoting Jesus of Nazareth

"We eat light, drink it in through our skins."
   Quoting James Turrell, a 20th–21st century American artist whose media it was to work in light

"The principal person in a picture is light."
   Quoting Edouard Manet, 19th century painter

"Information is light. Information in itself, about anything, is light."
   Quoting Tom Stoppard, 20th century playwright/screenwriter

"Science is spectral analysis. Art is light synthesis."
   Karl Kraus,19th–20th century Austrian playwright/journalist/poet

"Do not go gentle into that good night. Rage, rage against the dying of the light."
   Dylan Thomas, 20th century Welsh poet and writer

Dr. Arthur Zajonc explains, in his book *Catching the Light*, "Besides an outer light and eye, sight requires an 'inner light,' one whose luminance complements the familiar outer light and transforms raw sensation into meaningful perception. The light of the mind must flow into and marry with the light of nature to bring forth a world.

This urges us on a second inquiry. Having introduced the light of the mind, what, in fact, is the light of nature?"[13]

Light, he frequently points out, is itself required for seeing, but our eyes aren't able to actually see light itself. We experience the phenomenon of the existence of light. But light has no meaning to us until we "transform raw sensation into meaningful perception."

The physical and a metaphorical necessity for recording raw sensation onto an image—either on film or on digital media—appears to be extremely important to humans. Vitally important.

Chapter Notes:

12. A fundamental theory of matter and energy that explains facts that previous physical theories were unable to account for, in particular the fact that energy is absorbed and released in small, discrete quantities (quanta), and that all matter displays both wavelike and particle like properties, especially when viewed at atomic and subatomic scales.
Quantum mechanics suggests that the behavior of matter and energy is inherently probabilistic and that the effect of the observer on the physical system being observed must be understood as a part of that system. Also called quantum physics, quantum theory. *The American Heritage© Science Dictionary*. (2005) United States of America. Houghton Mifflin Company.

13. Zajonc, A. (1993). *Catching the Light: The Entwined History of Light and Mind*. New York, NY. Bantam Doubleday Dell Publishing Group, Inc. and Oxford University Press.

A portion of stained glass window on the Tabernacle Church in Beaufort, South Carolina, overlooking the resting place of Robert Smalls. During the American Civil War, he became a hero when he (as an enslaved African American) steered a ship out of Confederate-held Charleston and delivered it to Union troops.

THINK LIKE AN ARCHEOLOGIST

"See, said (Liberty Hyde) Bailey, how the leaves of this small plant stand forth extended to bathe themselves in the light... These leaves will die. They will rot. They will disappear into the universal mold. The energy that is in them will be released to reappear, the ions to act again, perhaps in the corn on the plain, perhaps in the body of a bird. The atoms and the ions remain or resurrect; the forms change and flux. We see the forms and mourn the change. We think all is lost; yet nothing is lost. The harmony of life is never ending. The economy of nature provides that nothing be lost."

Russell Lord, *Care of the Earth*

Archeology is the study of human history through the physical excavation of significant sites wherein artifacts, as well as other remnants, are uncovered and examined to discover information about the people who inhabited the site at a specific time.

Snapshot Archeology is the study of an individual's history through the visual excavation of significant, personal images—particularly snapshots—wherein artifacts, as well as other remnants, are uncovered and examined to discover information about the people whose likenesses were captured at a specific time.

Here are the abilities, tools and skills you'll be developing in Snapshot Archeology. Most of them are the same primary competencies utilized by archeologists in their work.

1. Curiosity

2. Investigative skills

3. The ability to identify a site (a snapshot) that has potential to yield interesting artifacts

4. A preliminary reference guide for identification of artifacts (symbols, patterns, colors, forms, numbers) provided for you on page 79

5. Critical thinking to separate the primary artifacts from the less informative ones

6. Visual mapping of your artifacts

7. Artifact documentation

8. Analytical skills to interpret your excavated data

9. Journal entries to interpret your individually generated data

10. Develop conclusions based on the synthesis of your excavated data and individual observations

1. Curiosity

You already possess this attribute to some extent. You wouldn't have been drawn to this book in the first place if you didn't have a natural curiosity and strong personal desire to find out if there are indeed messages hidden in your personal photographs.

True curiosity embodies an analytically-based avenue for inquiry while also leaving the door open for surprise and wonder to walk through.

You owe it yourself to allow the wisdom of the ages to freely meander around as you enter into the realm of signs, symbols, patterns and forms. We're all products of our environments. That fact doesn't have to stop us from being curious about details we've been overlooking for years. Expanding your capacity to be curious will have beneficial effects that will spill over into a great many other areas of your life.

Below are two quotes by notable people who incorporated curiosity into their lives and gave it free reign.

"I think, at a child's birth, if a mother could ask a fairy godmother to endow it with the most useful gift, that gift would be curiosity."
Eleanor Roosevelt

"The important thing is not to stop questioning. Curiosity has its own reason for existing."
Albert Einstein

---

2. Investigative Skills

The most popular fiction and nonfiction books, movies and television programs of all time are those featuring a detective of some description whose prime directive is to solve a mystery. The entire 300 pages or 120 minutes hinge on the skills of the story's hero to "crack the case"—to assemble clues to see the coherent "picture" instead of the jagged, disconnected pieces he or she stumbled across when the saga began.

We couldn't even begin to count the number of these types of stories we've ingested into our brains over our lifetimes. Just consider this for a moment: Every tale you've ever read or watched with this theme was about somebody else's story. You're about to become the detective in your own history's mystery. You're embarking on an exciting mission to unearth the hidden clues and camouflaged messages embedded in your personal snapshots.

What will you discover?

What mysteries will you solve?

Will more questions arise?

Here's what the world's most famous detective has to say on the subject of investigation:

"The world is full of obvious things which nobody by any chance ever observes."
Sherlock Holmes, quoted from *The Hound of the Baskervilles*

"You see, but you do not observe. The distinction is clear."
Sherlock Holmes, quoted from *A Scandal in Bohemia*

3. The ability to identify a site (a snapshot) that has potential to yield interesting artifacts

Wherever your snapshots are presently residing is the place to begin your search. Throw your inner critic out the window (along with whomever's voice that critic may use) concerning the state in which you find your images. This isn't the time to begin categorizing your photos. You're on a hunt. You're taking stock of which picture will provide useful data when you "dig" down into it.

Life itself is messy. When an archeologist gets a tip on an area he or she would like to explore, it's approached in the condition it is in at that time. The site is accepted exactly where it's located. It's inspected just as it is.

You might already have an image in mind to explore. That's fine. But if you have to search to locate a photograph that will serve you, one of the pitfalls you may encounter at this stage is the emotional aspects that sifting through your personal snapshots might ignite. This is your opportunity to shift the various feelings that arise within you by honoring your images with profound respect. You'll certainly experience the enormous energy I've been referring to throughout this book. There are very good reasons we keep our personal snapshots safely tucked inside boxes and carefully nestled between the pages of a closed album. They pack a powerful punch to our emotional system.

A positive way to deal with potentially overwhelming memories is to make sure you approach your selection process with the eye of a scientist. Before you look through your images, set up an area that is more "clinical." Perhaps you might go to a friend's house that takes you out of your comfort zones. Don't, for example, play music that inflames memories about the past. Don't spend inordinate amounts of time on one image.

The chapter in Part Three called "The GUT Gauge" will step you through the process of choosing a snapshot to explore. Avoid potential "pythons" if you can.

> *"I saw what looked like another fallen tree in front of me and put my foot on it to cross over. At that moment it reared up in front of me—the biggest python I had ever seen!"*
> Louis Leakey, British paleoanthropologist and archeologist, 1903–1972

---

4. A preliminary reference guide for the identification of artifacts (symbols, patterns, colors, forms, numbers) such as the guides beginning on page 79

Once you begin to investigate your snapshots, how will you know what you're looking for?

Archeologists use reference guides to help them identify the artifacts they discover related to their site. When, for instance, an archeology team explores the ancient Mayan city of Chichen Itza on the northern Yucatán Peninsula, they have a visual reference guide that provides them with information about previous finds both at the site they're investigating and at other Mayan digs.

Symbols have universal meanings. In fact, there are many basic shapes that have been recorded throughout history. I've provided simple, easy to read, guides for you to refer to beginning on page 79.

At the top in the above illustration: A list of Mayan numerals 0–19.
Bottom left: Maya glyphs in stucco from the Museo de sitio in Palenque, Mexico. (Wikipedia)
Bottom right: A detail of *Presentation of Captives to a Mayan Ruler*, c. A.D. 785; Usumacinta River Valley; Kimbell Art Museum Fort Worth, Texas. (Wikipedia)

5. Employ critical thinking to separate the primary artifacts from the less informative ones

When you begin to locate shapes and forms within your images, you'll have to use critical thinking skills to determine which of the artifacts you're finding will actually be useful in your final analysis.

After archeologists have spent time deciding where their shovels are going to be inserted into a patch of earth, they're relatively sure the soil they'll turn over will contain fragments of artifacts. Perhaps it will be a piece of a handle from a cup. Or maybe a corner of a fresco. It's altogether possible they'll find an intact artifact. But most of the time it will be small pieces of an article from antiquity.

Two examples of fragments unearthed during the preliminary excavation phase of a 17th century naval fort in Beaufort, S.C. The archeologists will catalog these pieces and compare them to others in a reference guide so they can identify their origins.

I'm always delighted by the reaction of the archeologists I've been fortunate enough to observe and photograph. Each time they sift through the contents of yet another shovel full of dirt, their eyes first widen with wonder; their mouths twitch as they sort through their mental laboratory, and then they focus their gaze on whatever they've unearthed with a laser-like precision. Their brains are also "sifting" through the artifacts they've encountered before, whether they've seen them personally or have run across them in related reference material. Their minds are chugging away to correctly categorize these, at times, tiny fragments of wood, stone or pottery, into a larger overarching story within its historical context.

They might not, after their on-the-fly analysis, decide that the fragment they've found is worth very much at all. They might choose to enter its discovery into their working journal to later determine if it's valuable. The archeologists pictured on the previous page actually placed the fragments into a paper bag, wrote down pertinent information about them on the bag and placed it back into the hole they'd dug. They were conducting their preliminary research for a later, more intensive exploration of the site.

The aspect to appreciate here is to be aware that your mind will be engaged in the critical thinking phase of the Snapshot Archeology process. You'll be crunching incoming data in many of the same ways as the scientists I've accompanied on their digs. You'll take the information you uncover, compare it to the possible definitions provided by your reference guide, think critically (intentionally) about whether or not your findings can be incorporated into the overarching history of the image, and then either choose to use the data, document it for later or disregard it altogether.

6. *Visual mapping of your artifacts*

The visual mapping of the symbols and other artifacts you discover in your snapshots is perhaps the most exciting phase of Snapshot Archeology. Different people have an affinity for different steps of the process, but I think my vote goes to this exercise.

There are probably as many ways to "map" images as there are individuals who'll engage in the process. I've experimented with a lot of ideas over the years. Some images have to be examined in special ways so I'm always open to hearing (and seeing!) the variety of modes to indicate the location of unique artifacts.

On these two pages are three examples of *visual mapping*. I'll go into greater detail about how you can develop your own style of mapping your images in Part Three.

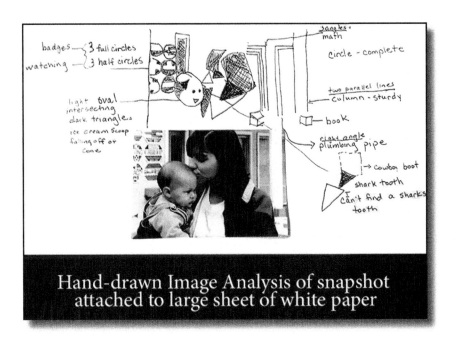

Hand-drawn Image Analysis of snapshot
attached to large sheet of white paper

Just prepare yourself for excitement and revelation to merge as you begin to intentionally regard a particular shape or form you observe in your photo. You'll identify it and then make a specific notation by tagging it in a way you'll recognize later during the process of analyzation. At this stage, you'll start to become aware of faint whispers of the potential message embedded in the snapshot. You also may notice that there's another pattern or a type of "mirror" arrangement appearing. Each image is singular and unique so it's difficult for me to be able to predict what may show up in your personal photographs.

Now, in response to your attention to it, the wave-particle expression of light begins to interact with you. Frequently as you're examining one part of your image, another pattern or shape that you hadn't consciously noticed before will "bubble up" in what can best be described as an aspect of your peripheral vision. You'll witness it become visible, but you won't be able to explain why you didn't see it in the first place. I find this the most challenging aspect to describe when people ask me to tell them about Snapshot Archeology. There aren't actually words to define the experience. A person simply has to go through the practice to see it. Then one can understand when I say that it's a difficult task to attempt to define.

There are obscure details of a snapshot that will literally appear as you behold the image.

Above: Archeologists make notations to visually map an excavated portion of a 19th century pottery site in South Carolina where they've unearthed artifacts.

7. *Manual entry (in a notebook or journal) or digital artifact documentation*

Once you've mapped the elements you notice in your image, it's time to begin the first step in the analyzation process.

Decide how you'd like to write down a list of the shapes, colors, forms, patterns and/or numbers you've mapped on your image.

I love checklists but I also love discovering how to do something in my own way. Sometimes, however, if I find myself stuck—I'll wish I'd read the instructions first. Other times, I'm happy I didn't.

Below is a copy of the form I use to keep track of the elements and artifacts I map in snapshots. You can download the PDF of the Snapshot Archeology Artifact Worksheet by visiting www.ChristiKoelker.com/snapshot-archeology/. Or create one of your own.

ARTIFACTS FOUND IN IMAGE/SNAPSHOT						DATE
Keep	ID/Area on Image	Symbol	Form	Color	Number	Other
☐						
☐						
☐						
☐						
☐						
☐						
☐						
☐						
☐						
☐						
☐						
☐						
☐						
☐						
☐						
☐						
☐						
☐						

You might want to consider keeping all your Snapshot Archeology explorations in a dedicated notebook or album. At times, I wish I'd kept all my image analyses in a uniform journal or album. My skills improved from the time I started visually mapping snapshots and developed considerably as I was able to make more symbolic connections. It would be nice to have a record to follow my evolution throughout the years and it would be helpful in sharing the maturation process of the technique. However, much to my chagrin, I'm not as organized as I'd like to be when it comes to keeping track of my own progress. I'm the kind of person who recognizes that I'm already deep in the middle of learning something and implementing it before I realize I've neglected to document it. Which makes it sort of out of character that I'm a documentary filmmaker. Of course, it's an historical documentary of somebody else's life, so maybe I'm safe.

I also ended up gravitating more toward analyzing my photos digitally using an image editor. I use Photoshop. However, sometimes I print out a snapshot because the particular image seems to want to offer more data through a tactile analysis. Other times, I go through the entire process on my computer screen. I have both a laptop and a desktop. Each of them has various versions of Photoshop on them.

I simply look at the image/snapshot and decide how I want to map it because as I've stressed over and over: this is your process. I'm walking you through the ways I've found work for me.

8. *Analytical skills to interpret your excavated data*

You'll turn up lots of information and what we're calling "artifacts" as you examine your chosen snapshot. This is the second half of entering what you've found in your image onto your chart. I reported in the previous step that you'll get very excited when you see shapes, patterns and forms revealing themselves to you. You'll be tempted to skip this part of the process and jump straight into interpreting them.

However, I've discovered that this part of the operation is an important aspect of the journey.

Let me explain.

Not everything you first notice in your image is worth exploring. You definitely shouldn't heavily edit yourself while you're intentionally examining your photo. Map everything you observe when you see it. You could look at it like a Saturday hike on a forest trail.

As you walk along, you look all around you. You notice the rocks, the clouds, the trees, the wildlife. You appreciate the whole experience. When you return home, you can't possibly make a list of everything you observed on your trek. Certain elements will stand out more than others in your mind as significant. If you take a little time to connect them mentally with a few memories and interpretations throughout the course of your life, you'll construct a personally meaningful interior story of what might appear to a passerby as just a nice walk in the woods.

Mapping each detail that appears in your image is the very much the same sort of experience. The things you saw on your walk are very beautiful, possibly fascinating. But when you finally link them with your interpretations, everything single thing you turn up in your initial investigation won't all tie into the final message you receive.

I think of this step as separating the non-essential elements from the principal ones. You'll understand this more completely as we move through the final two steps. For now, take my word that you'll be more satisfied with your final interpretations if you drop a few of the extraneous or partial shapes and forms at this point in the process.

That's not to say that partial forms and configurations aren't aspects of the complete message. You can always revisit the image to reassess your analysis. In fact, you'll find that you'll look back and forth quite naturally between the elements you've uncovered and the image you're analyzing. Keep in mind that I'm attempting to walk you through a technique I use and one which will become easier for you each time you practice it. There are not unbreakable rules to any part of it. Your personal interaction will evolve and you'll become increasingly intuitive the more often you read your photographs.

Make an initial decision on which form you want to use to write down what you've discovered. It can be something as simple as a sheet of notebook paper with numbers beside the element that correspond to the mapping method you used in #7 or as organized as a spreadsheet of some kind.

Again, the point of the exploration is for you to decode the messages hidden in your personal photographs. Your particular method of logging what you observe is strictly up to you. We all process information differently. I like to say there are those of us who read the instructions and those of us who barrel right on into whatever situation we find ourselves. I've decided I'm both of those people at different times.

9. *Journal entries to interpret your individually generated data*

Journaling is one tool you can employ to record your impressions of what you observe in your images, either during your excavation or later. Sometimes it seems to me the joy of journaling has become a little highbrow. There are more stylish, funky and artistic notebooks on the market than ever before in history. You can literally match the appearance of the cover and the weight of the paper inside it to your personality or moods. And I must admit that I'm a sucker for them.

I've never actually bought a Moleskin notebook but I've certainly picked them up to admire more than once. I always have several journals going at the same time because I love the feel of a good pen gliding along on paper. I have stacks of them in my office that I refer to now and then. I always feel more like a scientist writing down observations of the events in my life rather than an individual capturing her emotions. Although, over the course of my life, there've been a great many pieces of sentimental and sensitive entries in my journals. Mostly though, they hold my expressions about what I saw or thought about a particular situation. A snippet of an overheard conversation I didn't want to forget. The color of the sky or sea. When I go back and read particular entries (many of which were scribbled down quickly and without regard to form) I can clearly see a thread running through the writing. There's a wisdom in it as a collective that is beyond anything I intended in a hurried moment. That's probably because I didn't set out to capture the big picture at all. I was just recording snippets of the things I observed in myself and in the world around me in a similar manner to the way we're now considering writing down your observations of the elements you find in your images.

I'm bringing up my response to the word "journal" because that's simply the way I perceive it. It's vital that you decide the method that fits for you to record your own impressions of the artifacts when you get a "hit" in your "GUT Gauge."

That term will be explained thoroughly at the beginning of the very next section.

Also, the recognition you're hoping to elicit will reveal itself within your review of the information you bring forth from your personal responses. Each individual entry is akin to a sentence that, when you link them all together, will explain something to you about the image you're examining. It's within this phase of the process that you'll understand the action by which your images communicate with you. You'll figure out, first-hand, what I mean when I say your snapshots will "talk back to you."

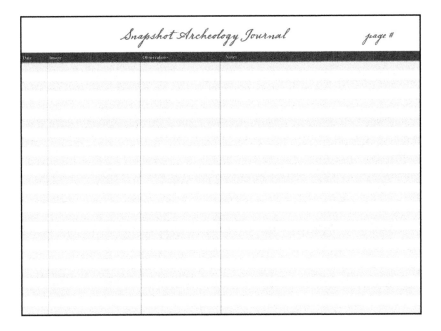

I have used form this as a printed, three-hole punched report to accompany snapshot readings I do for people in person. You can download the journal page shown above at www.ChristiKoelker.com/snapshot-archeology/.

10. *Develop conclusions based on the synthesis of your excavated data and individual observations*

Certainly this final step in the process is combined with the previous step. In fact, it's an extension of the journal entries you made from your observations of the artifacts you identified in the image you've been excavating. It's at this point—the conclusion—when you're going to connect the dots (so to speak).

Among the observations you've made are feelings, memories, intuitions and guidances inside yourself. Some of them have presented as mental images. Probably some of them have manifested as physical feelings. There's a distinct possibility that both of those perceptions have intermingled. Now you're called to interpret what you recognize as meaningful, linked information by the artifacts/elements you found in your image.

Surprisingly, this is often easier to explain than to write. Most smartphones have audio recording applications (apps) that come standard in their software. The reason I prefer this method for making first conclusions is that, as distant as our visual (right brain) and speech (left brain) centers are during aspects of analyzing our images; they somehow work very well together at this step.

As you start to explain to yourself what you've uncovered, more and more meaning will be siphoned to the surface. It doesn't matter if you stumble over your words. It makes no difference if you laugh or cry or say "uh" a hundred times. Nobody has to ever hear what you say except you.

I can also tell you that hearing yourself explain the connections you're making is very powerful as well. It's a bit like hearing your spirit's real voice for the first time.

The image will indeed be offering up a message (or several) and if you take your attention off of the snapshot to write down a thought, the connection may be weakened—if not lost. When I do private image readings for people, I follow all of the steps I've outlined in this section. I list the elements and artifacts I see on paper, as well as observations and interpretations. But when I offer a conclusion, I must do it verbally. I'll have the client respond to my analysis because, as I've tried to say over and over, ultimately they (you) are the only people who can understand the message being conveyed to them (you) in the image being excavated.

Let's revisit the reasons why you're the only one who can accurately decipher the messages in your images again. It's really important to remember these points as you craft your conclusion:

- You're the only one of you on the planet.

- Your experiences, perspectives, interactions and context are exclusive to you.

- No other being on earth can exist inside your frame of reference.

- You interpret elements (experiences, relationships, historical events) uniquely.

- You bring your singular self to the examination of the image you're excavating.

- Although another person may be able to identify some of the artifacts in the image you're excavating, they ultimately are not capable of seeing them through your "lens."

- You'll "add up" the elements or "connect the dots" between the artifacts to see a completely individual and unique message meant for you alone.

Don't stress about getting everything done exactly as you see it explained here. Seeing the messages in your photographs is a practice. You'll hone your vision to see more each and every time you interact with your images. You'll also find yourself being much more present within your daily environment. You don't really have to even try very hard. You'll naturally find yourself seeing shapes more clearly, colors more vividly and the interaction of them all more organically.

I was enchanted to discover—ultimately—that the greatest gift of this process is to engage in the strange obsession we have as humans to try and stop time in an image.

As my photographer hero, Dorothea Lange, said,

"The camera is an instrument that teaches people to see without a camera."

So, I would most reverently add, is a snapshot.

Sitting on the floor with my Grandmother Syble, and my cousins Sandy and Sheri, in about 1980. She's telling us the stories of her life as she's reminded of them by the snapshots she's showing us.

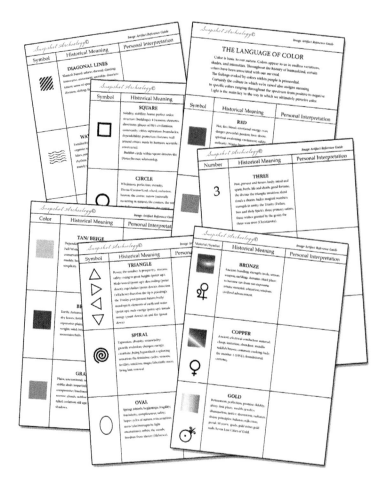

Image Artifact Reference Guides

TOOLS FOR YOUR
SNAPSHOT ARCHEOLOGY KIT:
SYMBOLS AND THEIR MEANINGS

"Cosmos is a Greek word for the order of the universe. It is, in a way, the opposite of chaos. It implies the deep interconnectedness of all things. It conveys awe for the intricate and subtle way in which the universe is put together."

Carl Sagan

There are hundreds—if not thousands—of websites and reference books explaining the meaning of signs, symbols, colors, shapes and numbers. I've used many of them myself over the years, including ancient and sacred texts, to come up with a simple reference for the rest of us. It's not my intention to be the absolute and final expert on the meanings of various elements. I needed a quick reference to use for myself when I'm examining my images. The chart that follows is the one I use (along with additional material) to help me puzzle out the messages in my photos.

Throughout history there have been basic symbols pecked into basalt rock as petroglyphs and carved onto the walls of stone caves as guidance. They have survived for millennia. A plethora of information, clues and stories have been left by the ancient Middle-Eastern cultures of Sumer and Egypt, Babylonia and Mesopotamia—as well as by the indigenous peoples from the North and South American cultures of the Maya, the Hopi and the Anasazi. Each color has a particular vibrational energy within the light spectrum.

Rarely do we recall that these are the elements of our precious earth; the universe in which our home resides and the cosmos with which we are just beginning to become acquainted. We're connected to the entire system. Humans are 65% oxygen, 18.5% carbon, 9.5% hydrogen, 3.3% nitrogen and 3.7% calcium, phosphorus, potassium, sulfur, chlorine, sodium, magnesium, iodine, iron and zinc. We are made of star dust, sharing the cosmic stage with the rest of creation.

How would we speak to our future selves, our cosmic descendants, if it were not through the timeless language of symbols? I've attempted to distill the major meanings attached to each symbol, number and color throughout history. Some of them will have meanings that will appear to be at odds with one another.

As you look at your images, you're going to see shapes or colors that will instantly resonate in a particular way. You'll record those as observations. Then later you'll sort them out using these reference guides together with your own analyses.

THE IMAGE ARTIFACT REFERENCE GUIDES

Symbols	pages 79–83
Lines	84–85
Colors	86–91
Metallics & Glass	92–96
Numbers	97–99

If a meaning I've listed doesn't work for you then go research it. It's a very simple thing to enter "the meaning of (fill in the blank with the symbol, number, sign or shape you're researching)" in the search engine of your choice.

Follow your intuition.

This is about you after all. You're connected to these ancient symbols and forms. You've seen them all your life.

It's the time to discover and recognize them as the building blocks of our deepest foundations of human communications.

Symbol	Historical Meaning	Personal Interpretation
	SQUARE Solidity; stability; home; perfect order; structure (buildings); 4 (seasons; elements; directions; phases of life); civilization; community; cities; separation; boundaries; dependability; protection (fortress; wall around cities); made by humans; scientific: constructed. ***Buddist***: circle within square denotes the Divine/human relationship.	
	CIRCLE Wholeness; perfection; eternity; Divine/Creator/God; wheel; inclusion; heaven; the center; nature (naturally occurring in nature); the cosmos; the sun; the full moon; completion; the center; the universe; bracelet; ring.	
	CROSS (X) Totality; relief; salvation; addition; communication between heaven and earth; protection from evil; facing a crossroads; orientation/intersection; space and time intersecting; safety (Red Cross); intersection; the sun; the moon; completion; perfection; the Christian faith; the center ; exclusion; "NO"; treasure ; delete; cross out.	

Symbol	Historical Meaning	Personal Interpretation
	TRIANGLE Power; the number 3; prosperity; success; safety; rising to great heights (point up); blade/sword (point up); descending (point down); cup/chalice (point down); direction (whichever direction the tip is pointing); the Trinity; past/present/future; body/mind/spirit; elements of earth and water (point up); male energy (point up); female energy (point down); air and fire (point down)	
	SPIRAL Expansion; divinity; immortality; growth; evolution; changes; energy; creativity; being hypnotized; a spinning sensation; the feminine; cycles; seasons; fertility; intuition; magic; labyrinth; maze; being lost; renewal.	
	OVAL Spring; rebirth; beginnings; fragility; femininity; completeness; safety; hope; cycles of nature; reincarnation; auras (electromagnetic light emanations); orbits; the womb; freedom from slavery (Hebrews).	

Symbol	Historical Meaning	Personal Interpretation
	RECTANGLE Order; geometry; conformity; familiarity; stability; commonness; rationality; formality; peacefulness; many of the same qualities as squares; used less often symbolically than squares.	
	CRESCENT *Waxing Crescent* (horns to left in Northern Hemisphere, right in Southern Hemisphere) young; growth; manifestation; attainment; expression; revelation; appearance of dreams; new beginnings; rebirth. *Waning Crescent* (horns to right in Northern Hemisphere, left in Southern Hemisphere) old; surrender; quitting; withdrawing; yielding; the end of a cycle.	
	DIAMOND Creation; reflection (one triangle reflected by another); connection; ownership; partnership; passageway; petal; strength; invincibility; secrets; spinning; hidden knowledge; protection; promise of matrimony.	

Symbol	Historical Meaning	Personal Interpretation
	5 SIDED STAR Pentagram; Star of Bethlehem; descent of spirit into matter; the Divine in humans; presence of God on earth; visitation of angelic beings; fidelity; constancy; light; loyalty; night; faith; love; Eastern Star (Adah, Ruth, Esther, Martha, Electra); North Star; guiding star; FATAL (fairest among thousands: altogether lonely).	
	6 SIDED STAR Hexagram; the merging of two triangles; connection of upper and lower dimensions; 6 directions of space; divine union of male (Shiva and female (Shakti); Star of David (Jewish tradition); Anahata (Sanscrit); unhurt, unbeaten, unbeaten; chariot/cart; protection; portal; spinning motion; unmanifest and manifest together; merkaba (sacred geometry/platonic solid).	
	ANCHOR Ground oneself; plant oneself; brace oneself; secure; support; hope; grip; control; to land somewhere; mooring in a storm; go ashore; stay put; adventure at sea; steadfastness; marine;	

Symbol	Historical Meaning	Personal Interpretation
	MANDORLA (*Vesica Piscis*) Two circles coming together; almond-shaped; interactions; interdependence; intersection of heaven (spirit) and earth matter); portal; passage-way; birth canal; shining aura around the heads of saints and holy figures; that area in which spiritual/sacred beings are enveloped; halo; basis for Christian fish symbol; unity; healing; restoration; internal spiritual light.	
	FLEUR DE LIS Flower; importance of tradition; influence of royalty; under protection; Virgin Mary; lily; lotus; Medieval French/European; decorative shape; weapon; crown; Holy Trinity; displaying Old World heraldry; influence of Old World in Contemporary World.	
	CADUSEUS Harmony; balance; authority; carried by couriers for safe passage; healing; physician; medicine; Herald's Wand; Hermes (Greece); Mercury (Roman); Rod of Asculapius (Greek -no wings); Aesculapian Snakes (Greek and Roman myths) that are non-venomous symbols of medicine.	

THE LANGUAGE OF LINES

Lines are points in space that move in a direction in a photographic image. Every line has a certain length, thickness, and bearing.

There are literal lines which exist in nature (such as lines on a zebra) and implied lines on and around the edge of forms.

The directions in which lines are arranged communicate particular feelings and information.

Symbol	Historical Meaning	Personal Interpretation
	**HORIZONTAL LINES** The horizon; the place where the sky meets the earth; passivity; gravity; perfect order; stability; calmness; tranquility; acceptance; repose; death; crops; physical matter as opposed to spiritual); quiet; organization.	
	VERTICAL LINES Powerful; height; grandeur; pillars; columns; imposing; growth; spirituality; integrity; churches; cathedrals; permanent; rising; dominance; inventory.	

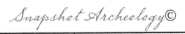

Symbol	Historical Meaning	Personal Interpretation
	DIAGONAL LINES Slanted; biased; askew; skewed; slanting; transverse; movement; unstable; disorientation; sense of speed (steeper = faster); division; sliding; falling; dynamic motion.	
	WAVY LINES Familiarity; comfort; relaxing; natural; organic; waters; (ocean; rivers; streams; lakes; ponds); waves; heat; music; long hair; rhythm; harmony; immortality; approximately equal to (tilde ~)	
	ZIG ZAG LINES Sharpness; harshness; heat; confusion, inspirations; rambling; changes; water; serpentine (snake-like); wandering; transformation; growth; variation; rain; fertility; lightning (vertical); broken (vertically).	

THE LANGUAGE OF COLOR

Color is basic to our nature. Colors appear to us in endless variations, shades, and intensities. Throughout the history of humankind, certain colors have been associated with our survival.

The feelings evoked by colors within people is primordial.

Certainly the culture in which we're raised also assigns meaning to specific colors ranging throughout the spectrum from positive to negative.

Light is the main key to the way in which we ultimately perceive color.

Symbol	Historical Meaning	Personal Interpretation
	RED Hot; fire; blood; emotional energy; war; danger; powerful; passion; love; desire; spiritual awakening; excitement; safety; authority; Winter berries; luck; prosperity. *Root chakra:* promotes grounding and centering. Main element: earth. Located at the base of the spine	
	ORANGE Warm/hot; joy; sunshine; strength; ambition; enthusiasm; happiness; success; creativity; exploration; affordability; Autumn; Halloween; harvest. *Sacral chakra:* promotes energy and creation. Main element: water Located in the lower abdomen	

Color	Historical Meaning	Personal Interpretation
	YELLOW Warm; light; sunshine; intellect; perception; happiness; flowers; optimistic; activates memories; clarity; masculine; Fall leaves; Spring flowers; corn/maize; taxis; school buses; jealousy in France; sadness in Greece. *Sacral chakra:* promotes energy and positive charge. Main element: fire Located above the navel in the solar plexus	
	GREEN Warm-cool; nature; fertility; freshness; renewal; Spring; luck; rebirth; safety; self-respect; restful; wellbeing; well-balanced; connection; money; nausea; envy. *Heart chakra:* promotes compassion and love Main element: water Located in the center of the chest	
	BLUE Cool; truth; fidelity; trust; perceptiveness; expression; communication; feminine; sky and sea; loyalty; stability; creativity; arts; sleep; immortality; heaven; calm; reflection. *Throat chakra:* promotes expression and will power Main element: water Located in the throat	

Color	Historical Meaning	Personal Interpretation
	INDIGO Devotion; perception; depth; intuition; magic; mystery; high frequency vibration; wisdom; justice; grace; importance; wealth; inner mind; fairness. *Third Eye chakra:* promotes intuitive abilities and spiritual perception Main element: air Located in the center of the forehead	
	VIOLET Cool; peace; balance; guidance; idealism; sacrifice; wisdom; healing; spirituality; connection; inspiration; feminine; visionary; beauty; floral. *Crown chakra:* promotes enlightenment and unity Main element: air Located on the top of the head	
	PURPLE Cool and hot (combination of blue and red); royalty; faith; truth; patience; nobility; extravagance; connection to Spirit; children's favorite color; floral; mystery; food (grapes and plums).	

Color	Historical Meaning	Personal Interpretation
	PINK Tenderness; compassion; love; feminine; softness; caring; romantic; nurturing; Valentines; floral; internal; inflammation; liberal; sea shell; flamingo; combines energies of white and red.	
	WHITE Purity; sterility; cold; innocence; virginity; peace; cleanliness; perfection; simplicity; angelic; bride; snow; winter; ice; reverence; hospital; medicine; milk; high tech; contemporary. sacred animals (albinism).	
	IVORY Unification; purity; innocence; natural; cleanliness; neutral; pearl-essence; opaline; glowing; ancient; decoration; tusks; calm; elegance; refuge; seclusion; ivory tower.	

Color	Historical Meaning	Personal Interpretation
	TAN/ BEIGE Dependable; conservative; reliable; dull; Fall/Winter; neutral; earthiness; conservative; repressive; plain; drab; muddy; heavy weight; calmness; simplicity.	
	BROWN Earth; Autumn/Winter; organic matter; dry leaves; fertility; wood; conservative; repressive; plain; drab; muddy; heavy weight; solid; bricks; stable; mountains/hills.	
	GRAY Plain; unemotional; neutral; corporate; stable; drab; impartial; indecisive; compromise; loneliness; reserved; sorrow; clouds; neither black nor white; relief; isolation; old age; maturity; shadows.	

Color	Historical Meaning	Personal Interpretation
	BLACK Unknown; night; mourning; simplicity; elegance; mourning; grief; authority; depth; endless; contrast; infinity; endless; cave; mystery; heaviness; secrets; evil; contrast.	

THE LANGUAGE OF METALLICS AND GLASS

Metallic and glass substances are all around us. Plastics have replaced objects that were once crafted out of metals or glass and have contributed to harming the planet.

Alchemy was the ancient predecessor of modern chemistry. Practitioners experimented with transforming base metals - such as tin and lead - into precious metals like gold. The colors associated with metals also incorporate an aspect of light.

They're reflective and shiny. Noting the presence of metallics and reflective elements in your images opens up another path to understanding the messages embedded in your photographs.

Material/ Symbol	Historical Meaning	Personal Interpretation
	**PLAIN GLASS** Clear; perception; water; transparent; fragile: breakable; windows; seeing inside; not hidden; exposed;	
	STAINED GLASS Color; light; pattern; design; symbolic; dramatic; spiritual; embedded meaning.	

Material/Symbol	Historical Meaning	Personal Interpretation
	MIRRORED GLASS Reflection; copy; metallic; projection; recollections; water; the unconscious; narcissism (myth of Narcissus); threshold of reality between the conscious and the unconscious; knowledge in general; self-knowledge; scientific. The ANKH symbol from Eqypt.	
	ALUMINUM Energy; flight; travel; conductive; anti-corrosive; silvery-white metal; light weight; thermal; malleable; moldable; invention; alloy; combination; Mercury.	
	BRASS Alloy of copper and zinc; decorative; thresholds; openings (door knockers and knobs); connections; low friction; chaotic; youthful; impetuosity; healing; rejuve-nating; substitute for gold in ritual ceremony.	

Material/Symbol	Historical Meaning	Personal Interpretation
	PLATINUM Most precious metal; catalyst; success; jewelry; malleable; limited supply; will not tarnish; represents "over a million sold"; used in chemical laboratories; determination; fortitude.	
	SILVER Feminine; intuition; moon; stars; the ocean; artistic expression; intuition; second place; cleansing; balance; authority; speed; exchange; redemption; high technology; highest electrical conductivity.	
	ZINC Activator; enhancer; supporter of life; communication; male energy; makes way for changes; helps focus physical senses; recharger.	

Material/Symbol	Historical Meaning	Personal Interpretation
	BRONZE Ancient; bonding; strength; tools; armor; weapon; melding; Autumn; third place; to become tan from sun exposure; artistic material; education; wisdom; civilized advancement.	
	COPPER Ancient; electrical conduction material; cheap; imitation; abundant; metallic reddish brown; common; cooking; luck; the number 1 (ONE); foundational; currency.	
	GOLD Refinement; perfection; promise; fidelity; shiny; first place; wealth; jewelry; illumination; justice; decoration; radiance; divine principles; balance; reflection; greed; 50 years; goals; gold mine; gold rush; Seven Lost Cities of Gold.	

THE LANGUAGE OF NUMBERS

Numbers are much more than how many of one thing or another we count. They are a truly universal language. They are abstract concepts of the mind; yet materially physical at the same time. The relationship between the physical and non-physical in numbers is always in play. They are extremely venerated and powerful historic symbols.

Numerology is the application of the meaning of numbers to an event or situation. Mathematics is the study of topics such as quantity (numbers), structure, space, and change. Some claim certain numbers are "lucky" or "unlucky": sacred or profane.

Number	Historical Meaning	Personal Interpretation
1	**ONE** The best; the beginning; alone; confidence; the leader; the creator; strength; masculine; individuality; point of entry; point of contact; point of ignition; unity; action; purpose; solidarity; direction; focus; ambition; pillars; columns; vertical line.	
2	**TWO** A pair; partnership; balance; opposition; contrasts; duality; division; feminine; moon number; wisdom; good judgement; harmony and rivalry; yin and yang; karma; choice; attraction; heart shape; ear shape.	

Number	Historical Meaning	Personal Interpretation
3	**THREE** Past, present and future; body, mind and spirit; birth, life and death; good fortune; the divine; the triangle; intuition; third time's a charm; lucky; magical number; strength in unity; the Trinity (Father, Son and Holy Spirit); three primary colors; three wishes granted by the genie; the three wise men (Christianity).	
4	**FOUR** Four seasons; four cardinal directions (North, South, East, West); solid; stable; four earth elements (water, fire, air, water); four seasons (Spring, Summer, Winter, Fall); reason; reliability; structure; boundaries; protection; trust; home; fortress; foundation; box; office; safety; four-leaf clover=lucky; conventionality; rationalism.	
5	**FIVE** Human fives (five fingers, five toes); senses; a human figure with outstretched limbs; movement; enthusiasm; "high five" greeting; pentagram (two points down for Christmas star: two points up signifies devil); higher knowledge; health; light; guidance; beliefs; faithfulness.	

Number	Historical Meaning	Personal Interpretation
6	**SIX** Beauty; completeness; perfection; Venus; love; psychic knowledge (sixth sense); well-developed instinct; achieving balance; equality; truth; lighting the path forward; sincerity; balance; equalibrium; the cube; the Star of David; a hexagram; the winning throw in dice.	
7	**SEVEN** Connection to source; the Universe; Wonders of the World; days of the week; safety; rest; perfection; planets; musical tones; colors of the rainbow; progression; manifestation; synthesis; understanding; direction; poetry; song; rhythm; 7 circles form "The Seed of Life."	
8	**EIGHT** Infinity; endless; continuing forever; eternal; regeneration; resurrection; reincarnation; rebirth; completion; the whole; time and space; mystery; magic; perfect rhythm; abundance; power; decisiveness; solidarity; mandala (Hindus 8 x 8 - order of celestial world established on earth); octogon; stop.	

Number	Historical Meaning	Personal Interpretation
9	**NINE** Triple triad (3 x 3); completion; supreme power; heavenly number; two triangles coming together signifying the male, mountain, fire and female, water, cave. Wisdom; leadership; sacred knowledge; powerful magic; 9 fruits of the spirit (love, joy, peace, patience, kindness, goodness, faithfulness, gentleness, self-control); evolution; process; recognition; invention.	
0	**ZERO** Transformational change; empty; null; the cosmic egg; nothingness and totality in one place in space; the ultimate mystery; the eternal; the unmanifest; potential; possibility; rebirth; cycles; the container of everything; the center of the universe.	

✶ Whenever you're faced with multiple numbers, break them down into single digits. Then you'll better be able to consider their meaning in your image.

For example: the number 25 would simplify to 2 + 5. The number 7 would be the artifact for you to explore. The number 109 would simplify to 1 + 0 + 9 = 10. Take your sum of 10 and simplify it again. 1 + 0 = 1. The number 1 would be the artifact for you to explore.

USING THE GUT GAUGE
TO CHOOSE YOUR FIRST IMAGE

"You cannot teach a man anything!
You can only help him discover it for himself."

Galileo

I'm going to show you how to examine both an image on paper and a digital image. Again, there are several different methods I use for each of these ways of looking at my images, but at its heart, it's still basically the same process. We'll start at the same place because it always begins with your chosen image. First, you'll need to decide on one image from your collection you think and feel has the right combination of energetic components to compel you to proceed through the process of excavation.

Segments of this book have been written (and re-re-written) over a number of years. During that time, the various ways in which we capture and observe our images has morphed into the stuff of my childhood fantasies! No one can possibly be as delighted as I am to be living right here, right now in the first years of the 21st century. Of course I wish the world could be a more loving and infinitely kinder place than it seems to be at present. I meditate, pray and work toward those outcomes every single day. Yet, in terms of the technology we've been able to experience, we live in a fantastic time. It's nothing less than pure magic.

As we go along, I'll refer to the entire set of images you've amassed as your "collection," regardless of the sort of far-flung system (or non-system) it may be. If you doubt your images are some of your most valuable possessions consider that people whose homes have been destroyed by fire or other natural disasters report that the loss of their personal photographic "collection" was among the most devastating aspects of the catastrophe. Our personal images mean the world to us. They literally prove that our "world" happened as our reality. So as you embark on your journey to discover how this is true of your life as well: let down your guard a little bit. Open your mind to allow your preconceived concepts of where energy is stored and how it can be accessed to grow bigger. Expand your circle of perception to include some sources you might never have considered before.

Once you learn how to focus on various aspects of your images, you'll be able to, in turn, see them everywhere you look. Whether you're observing them on your cell phone camera, in the Cloud, on Dropbox, on Snapfish, on your iPad or in a framed photo hanging on the wall. It will make no difference. You'll find the expansion experience will naturally integrate your visual perception abilities into the movies you watch. Even art that was created centuries ago will take on a brilliance and an immediacy that you've never experienced before. All those outcomes stem from opening up to your "GUT Gauge." It's certainly not a new concept, but it's definitely an overlooked one that's been downgraded over the last few centuries. We've all been literally programmed to set it to the side while we listen to "experts" in every field tell (sell) us the products and services we really "need" to become "successful" people. If Newtonian-based science can't prove it or you can't buy it at Walmart, we've been wired to discard it as rubbish..

The path we'll take first is to find pictures that seem to "speak" to you. There may be just one small element that calls out, "Me! Pick me!" You've probably already been introduced to that exceptionally enthused voice. You might even have used a method similar to this if you've ever thumbed through magazines to pull pictures from them for a vision board or a collage. That scrappy sense of attraction is a gift from a part of our bodies that connects us viscerally to what we see, hear, touch, smell, and taste. It also has the capacity for quickly designating just which image calls to us and it's located in the area of our solar plexus. I've lovingly named it "The GUT Gauge."

Step One: Introducing Your GUT Gauge—Grace Underlying Thought

Your "gut reaction" is the umpire of the game constantly being played by your senses. You'll want to introduce yourself, make friends and respect this wise, ancient core of yourself. It will guide you toward finding the precise images you'll want to explore. Over the years, I've settled into referring to it as my "Grace Underlying Thought" Gauge. Better known to my friends and family by its nickname as my "GUT Gauge." It resides in what feels like (from a little pushing and prodding around the center on your torso) the hollow area between your belly and the upside-down "V" of your ribs. It's the spot where you feel the "butterflies" when you're excited or nervous. There area where you feel the literal "punch" in your center when bad news comes. Where you feel a "drop" when you're disappointed. Where you feel the "giddiness" when you're in love.

I was always confused as to the reason it took me such a long time to internally understand the concept of "grace." Eventually I began to figure out that I'd gotten the splendidly uncomplicated concept of what grace truly means tangled up with the guilt-laden ones from the religion of my childhood. And, although it pains me to admit, it took me more years than I care to ponder to allow myself to engage with grace in one of its simplest forms: as the easiest way to connect to the present. The gift of grace is that it's a present (as in a wrapped box with a big beautiful bow) of the present (as in right now at this very second) moment.

If it feels better or more comfortable for you, it's fine to substitute the word "gift" for "grace" while you're going through the process of choosing an image to examine. That substitution still allows the acronym (GUT) to work in the same way. Personally, I love the dynamism of the term "grace." It's a word for me that denotes movement. An energetic force. Something that's shared with me and provided for me from a source much bigger than myself. A communication delivered via the messages in my images, among other places, that makes its presence (presents) known right in the center of my body. That's the target of the frequency; the bull's-eye for the arrow.

Thousands, possibly millions—depending on your age—of the significant and meaningful actions we've taken in our lives were decided based on the wise guidance of this area in the center of our being. We're very familiar with the way our guts react to high-energy events. We say we "get butterflies in our stomachs" when we're nervous or excited. It describes the feeling of nausea or dis-ease when something goes against our basic nature. We hold on as it "drops" when we're disappointed or shocked.

In any case, it's best not to be stuck on a rational explanation or complex reason as to why you're drawn to choosing an image. I'm going to ask you to consciously disconnect your logical mind and choose images that physically pull toward you in the gut area of your body. You'll learn to submit to the magnetic attraction. That ability will develop relatively quickly.

The Biology of The GUT Gauge

The nerves in our gut (digestive system/gastrointestinal tract) are much more basic and instinctual than the ones which have evolved in our brains: a primal holdover from our distant human past.

Our GUT Gauge only knows "yes" or "no" whereas our everyday, occupied, reasoned mind will say, "I'll take this information and put it together with all the other data I've gathered to make a rational decision." Our brains are incredibly complicated sensory organs, but the powerful circuits in area of our the solar plexus are our instinctual instrument panels. It's located—conveniently—in the center of the core of our bodies just below our hearts (feeling, emotion) and just above our reproductive (creation) organs. A magnetic and dynamic central receiver.

Just surrender to the pure magnetism of the experience and trust it for this portion of the process. It's not in the least scary, but it's absolutely electrifying when you cooperate with it for the first time.

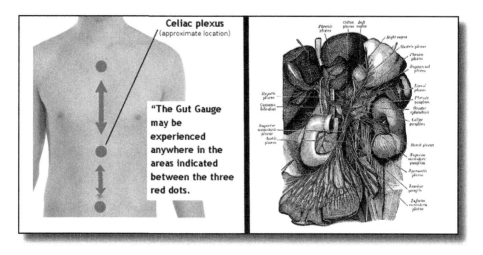

Science surrounding the GUT Gauge. The celiac plexus—or "solar plexus" because of its radiating nerve fibers—is a complex network of nerves (a nerve plexus) located in the abdomen, where the celiac trunk, superior mesenteric artery, and renal arteries branch from the abdominal aorta is located. It is located behind the stomach and the omental bursa, and in front of the crura of the diaphragm, on the level of the first lumbar vertebra. (Illustrations: Wikipedia.)

Step Two: Separating the Wheat from the Chaff

The second part of the process depends on creating several conditions to make choosing your first image a comfortable and productive experience for you. Begin by being on the lookout for a time when you're feeling happy and when you're physically well. In other words, don't try to go through piles of snapshots or folders full of digital images if you're under the weather. Just because you're you'll be home from work anyway doesn't mean you'll have your GUT Gauge working well enough to find an image to excavate. Please don't do on this on a day when you're feeling less than what you'd consider "good". Certainly not when you're still in the process of grieving a loss. Photographic images contain powerful energy. We tend to forget this very potent fact because we "consume" so many images in a day. The ways in which you can safely interact with your personal pictures depends on being in a relatively non-reactive state before you attempt to choose an image to explore.

This step can take as little as two hours but might stretch into as long as four or six. Or you may already have a particular image in mind. But if you need to sift through a few piles of photos, make sure the dog has been fed; the kids are at Grandma's house; your partner is out of town (or out for the day) or your elderly parent has plenty of diversions before you get started.

Look at your photos *alone*.

Suffice it to say that every person on the earth possesses his or her own individual energy. The only human energy you want to engage with the images you're perusing is yours. Honor this suggestion because it will allow you to be relaxed for the session.

In addition, you're going to need a space in which you'll be comfortable working yet also a place that offers a few flat surfaces to accommodate an area for sorting. Situate yourself so you're comfortable in your favorite chair, at a table or on the floor. Personally, I like to sort my paper photographs on my bed with my back up against the headboard for support. Come to think about it, I also sit on my bed with my laptop to select a digital picture.

Allow enough space around you so that you can make several piles of photos. Pour yourself a cup of tea, a smoothie or a tall mug of hot chocolate (whatever you most like to sip on when you're relaxing) before you start to go through the shoeboxes or old photo albums. Don't drink alcohol during this part of the process, as it will dilute your pure, intuitive abilities and heighten your emotional responses. Just your Spirit, and not the distilled kind, is invited to this dance at the party. That's the only one that should be in attendance right now.

Also, be careful not to play any music that elicits a heightened emotional response in you. For example, don't play Van Morrison's "Moondance" if it was the song that you and your recent ex valued as a couple. If you feel you just must have some background ambiance, find a CD or a YouTube.com channel with nature sounds. Or download something low key and nondescript such as John Grout's *Relaxing Sounds of Nature* or Chuck Plaisance and Suzanne Doucet's *Sounds of Nature Sampler*.

There's the white-noise of ocean sounds; the trickling of creeks or brooks; sounds of wind blowing through the trees. But for me, even those wild sounds stir my love of walking by the sea and my childhood memories of the sounds and smells of the woods. Sometimes, when I'm really wanting to pay attention to what I'm doing, I find my mind wandering all over the place and I get distracted because I remember walking on the beach at sunset or I want to stop doing the project at hand to go for a hike in the woods.

Remember the heads-up I gave you earlier? I told you that when you venture inside this world, which appears to be only about the messages in your personal snapshots, that you'll be coming up against lots of potent energies we generally take for granted? Can you understand what I'm prompting you to consider here?

We're entering a landscape of senses, emotions, symbols and feelings. It's a place we've always controlled in a tiny space that's been kept between the covers of a photo album or the borders of a snapshot. You're now paying attention and engaging your intention as you see your personal images. It's a little like opening Pandora's Box and yet it's a rich, whole-body, whole-spirit energy fest.

Now let's go back to choosing an image to explore.

Decide on a group of images with which to begin.

1. Pick up an album or a handful of photos…OR

2. Pull up a folder on your computer or laptop.

3. Pick up or look at each photo.

4. Scan it briefly with your eyes to expose it to your GUT Gauge.

5. View the picture as you would flash cards.

6. Pick up (or click on) a photo; glance at it and decide if it "speaks" to you, "grabs" your awareness, sends you "vibes" of any type or simply makes you curious.

   I find the images that are the most fun to work with are frequently the ones I'm just plain curious about the reasons it's still following me around after so many years. I know enough, by now, to suspect that there's a communication in there waiting for me.

7. Make a "yes" pile of preliminary photos and put the "no" photos back in the box or album from which they originally came.

This isn't the time to rearrange your pictures or make decisions on which ones of them you want to throw away. That's an entirely different operating system than the one you're employing right now. So fight the urge to organize.

This is also likely to be a somewhat emotional process since you'll come across images of people who were (are) dear to you or were (are) a challenge for you to view in photos. That's one of the major reasons you need to be in a good state of mind before you begin. The best advice for this potentially upsetting situation is to move on as fast as you can to the next image.

Shortlist to Choosing an Image to Excavate:

A. Take a single photo out or look at it on your screen; expose it to your GUT Gauge for an instant by glancing at it.

B. Let a "yes" or "no" bubble up into your awareness.

C. Then put the photo in the "yes" pile or back into the container from which it came if the answer is "no".

Make an effort to remain detached from the meaning the image would elicit from the "you" who existed in that past space in a past time. Remember to try to keep this in mind through any strong emotions rising to the surface during this culling process.

This beginning step is ultimately about what the image will reveal to you in the form of a message. You can't see the message if you're getting involved with the people pictured there or the situation depicted.

You have to try and stay in a somewhat disconnected state at this stage. Give all your choosing power over to your Grace Under Thought Gauge. It will protect you as it does its job of dependably steering you toward excavating your first image for hidden messages.

Here are a few more hints to guide you as you look at your personal photographic images:

1. Briefly determine the room or area where the picture was taken.

2. Quickly note the placement of people's hands and in which directions they're looking.

3. Where are you in the picture?

4. What are you wearing? Did you pick it out? Where did it come from?

5. If the photo was taken outdoors, are there compelling shapes that seem to immediately catch your eye in the trees, the clouds or the sky in the background?

Let the answers flash into your mind and make an instantaneous call as to whether this particular photo is a link in the chain or a dead end. It will become easier as you go along and you'll have a remarkable experience viewing your photos in this particular way.

I often compare it to being in a dark room with a strobe light going off every couple of seconds. As the strobe flashes, you'll see an image of a scene that's occurred in your life. Yet, somehow, it's disconnected from time or emotion. You'll recognize that the photographic recording was you, or someone else or a particular place. You'll be the observer of the play and not the actor.

"Learn how to see. Realize that everything connects to everything else."

Leonardo da Vinci

PART THREE: DIGGING IN

Congratulations! You've looked through your photo collection and hopefully decided on one image. And as I've said before, if you're is anything like I am, you have hundreds, possibly thousands, of paper images "filed" in various areas around your house—family photos, snapshots of friends, birthday parties, births, funerals, get-togethers and celebrations of all assorted flavors.

Maybe there are still other personal photos you want to consider. Maybe they're the ones you chose a long time ago. They're the ones that "made the cut" at some point and are tucked inside frames that hang on your wall. Or perhaps they're your most beloved ones that are sitting on your coffee tables and end tables?

Or resting on your beside tables?

Or tucked among the books and knick-knacks on shelves in your house or apartment?

And then there are the masses of digital images on your computer and phone camera.

Or in Dropbox.

Or in the Cloud.

Out of all of these many images, you and your GUT Gauge are charged with choosing *only one* to explore as we step through the Snapshot Archeology technique for the first time.

If it's not in digital form yet, I'll show you how to take it from the 3-D to the 2-D form in the very next section.

In any case, you're going on a journey with this particular photograph so buckle up and get ready for an extraordinary experience.

WORKING BY HAND
WITH ORIGINAL PAPER IMAGES

There are certain times when I prefer the tactile experience of excavating the messages in my snapshots. It feels to me like an art project. In fact it's just that!

This is the way I isolated the signs, symbols and clues when I first started doing more than seeing them with my eyes. I began finding methods to track the things I was noticing. I simply had fun looking and drawing. As a result, over several years, I discovered patterns and was able to connect events that had happened in the span of time since the photo was captured. This way of interacting with my photos connects all my senses in my physical body to something a little more ethereal. I get out my colored pencils, my acetate pages or tissue paper, my markers and a notebook so I can lose myself in the image for a while.

I use the same progression for moving through the process of discovery. Photographing and observing archeologists have given me a framework. Once again, these are the steps that always guide me.

1. Curiosity

2. Investigative skills

3. The ability to identify some element that has the potential to yield interesting artifacts

4. A preliminary reference guide for the identification of artifacts (symbols, patterns, colors, forms, numbers). Use the one provided in this book beginning on page 79

5. Critical-thinking to separate the primary artifacts from the less informative ones

6. Visual mapping of your artifacts

7. Artifact documentation

8. Analytical skills to interpret your excavated data

9. Journal entries to interpret your individually generated data

10. Conclusions based on the combination of your excavated and individual data

Interacting by hand is my favorite approach to Snapshot Archeology if I have time to play. The insights I experience when I handle my photographs is more internal and more expansive simultaneously. Sweeter somehow. And as in any hands-on, artistic practice, I feel myself connected to the unfolding of the final interpretation on a creative level as opposed to just an interpretive one.

When I'm finished and I look at the completed drawing of the shapes, forms, colors and artifacts I've traced with the pencils or markers in my hand, I discover a new image altogether.

As I've talked about before, I must use my own images because that's the key ingredient of beginning this sort of image investigation. I have to possess the feelings about the subject of the picture before I can discover the messages waiting for me. Anyone can use the same techniques I'm demonstrating and explaining in this book to find shapes and symbols in other people's images but the personal connection won't be as compelling.

TURNING YOUR PAPER IMAGE INTO A DIGITAL ONE

When you're attempting to work with a traditional 4 x 6 (and sometimes even smaller 3 to 3½ x 5 inches) black-and-white or color paper photograph, you'll discover that it's really too small to do any kind of practical manipulation or investigation. I have old snapshots from the 1950s that aren't much bigger than some of the thumbnail images I get back with the digital prints I've had developed at a retailer. Without any magnification, you're only able to see a very small part of the picture when you look at it with your naked eyeball. Believe me when I assure you that there's an incredible amount of information hiding under the surface of what appears as just an old, faded snapshot.

Throughout my photo escapades, during the years of navigating the changing landscape of analog photography and film to its current digital form, I've created a lot of prints that are quite large. Some of them are as big as 16 x 20 to 20 x 24 inches. I'll also show you the technique I use when working with the largest of prints. Sometimes there's no possible way to remove a large print from its frame without damaging the image, the matting, the material from which the frame is constructed or all of them. This isn't the most common type of print you'll be examining but it's nice to know you'll have the reference in this book if you ever wish to excavate a really big image.

The most important idea to keep in mind when you're working with any original image is that you don't want to cause any destruction or degradation. Remember, these are primary sources. They're historical documents. They're golden and they're valuable in exactly the state they're in at the present moment. You'll want to make a copy, in some safe, non-destructive way that preserves the condition of the original image. In other words, you're creating a copy that will allow you to work on another surface to unlock the messages inside the image without doing any damage to the unique photograph you've chosen to explore.

The very first step I take when I've decided on an image to inspect if I'm not working on a copy of a print by hand is to transform it into a digital file.

I can accomplish this in one of two ways.

1. Scan the image.

I've used a Canon scanner for years. It's traveled with me through three documentaries, scores of short projects, family reunions and interviews. I'm always nervous about bragging on how great it's performed since it could die at any moment (knock on wood and throw salt over my shoulder!). I think I love it so much because it was working with images reproduced on the Canon scanner that opened my eyes to the depth of information contained in most photographs. Recently I bought an Epson Workforce portable color document scanner that takes up less room in my travel case. So far, so good.

I've also been able to scan my old 35mm and 2¼ inch negatives and slides. Though the quality isn't perfect, I've still been able to zoom in and see aspects of the image that I wouldn't see otherwise. There's definitely better technology for scanning your negatives and slides, but I mention the process here because it can be done, to some degree, on a home-flatbed scanner.

Generally, it's possible to make a digital scan yourself, particularly if the original is no larger than about 8 x 10 or possibly 8½ x 11 inches. Those sizes will work with most home-use scanners. There are large flatbed scanners that allow you to make digital scans of larger images, but those are generally only available at brick and mortar stores such as Staples or Office Depot. Depending on where you live and your access to an office supply store or photo shop, you may find another business that'll offer the service. Almost all of the new printers released into the market in the past few years have a scanning bed incorporated into them that's also used when you want to make copies. The goal you're aiming for will be the same. You're transforming your paper print into a digital form.

There are two important points to remember when scanning your photos. First, make sure the scanner is set to capture the image in at least 300 DPI (dots per inch). Also, you'll want the resulting image in a digital form such as a jpeg or another file that's compatible with your computer image editing software. A higher resolution will insure that you'll have more data visible in your image for you to explore. A higher DPI produces a more detailed picture in the outputted print or digital image.

Depending upon the scanner type you're using, you'll be able to find the right way to set up your printer scanner either in the accompanying instruction manual or by searching for the manufacturer's website on the Internet. When all else fails, you can go to an office supply store and use their scanner. Or you can have them scan your photo for you. Just make sure to ask them to set the DPI to at least 300 or higher. Usually 600 DPI is the highest resolution you'll want to use. The higher the DPI, the larger the digital file will be. The larger the digital file, the more space it takes up in your computer.

Also it's a good idea to buy and present them with a portable USB drive on which they can store the digital image. They might also be able to email the file to you (if it's not too large to transmit) so you can download straight to your computer drive. There are always CDs, but it's a waste to use one for a single image unless you don't have any other way to access the digital data.

2. Take a photograph of the paper image.

This saves time and money if you already have a mobile phone with a built-in camera or a digital camera you can connect to your computer. I've used this method more times than I can count to grab an image in a museum or from a family member's collection while I'm interviewing them. It also allows you to copy an image larger than 8½ x 11 inches. The challenge facing you (and all of us) will be getting enough light on the image along with holding the camera/phone steady enough to prevent blurriness. There's nothing new about this form of making copies. It's the way painters and artists have documented their original pieces for decades.

One of the easiest ways to solve a lighting deficit is to photograph your piece outside during the day. It's possible to find a brightly-lit place in your house or apartment, but many times the amount of light is just not sufficient enough to get a crisp, clear copy. You'll have to go outside to expose it.

Your goal is to make a copy and not to damage the original. Make sure to lay out a piece of plastic before you place your picture on any kind of surface. You don't want to take a chance that moisture or dirt will compromise your image. Remember, you're a snapshot archeologist. Archeologists are scientists who take great care with every piece of history they touch. This image is a shard of historical data containing important information about your unique life on this planet. If water or dirt gets on the image, the original message will be compromised and you might never able to see it clearly. The data will be lost! The plastic can be a clean baggie, as long as it's larger than the image you're photographing.

Check that bright sunlight isn't shining directly on the image you intend to photograph. Consider where the light is emanating from at various times during the day. Indirect lighting is the type of illumination that will yield the best results. Indirect light, also called diffused light, can be found in areas where there are no singular shafts of light and an evenly distributed amount of bright illumination. An overcast day will generally provide a light that appears to be coming from all directions at once instead of from a single source. Some types of shade offer an indirect, diffuse lighting situation.

You might also experience glare from strong light bouncing off of the coating applied to preserve most paper images. Sometimes it's almost as difficult as photographing an image behind the glass in a frame. You might also consider that the exposure to UV light on an old photograph needs to be kept to a minimum. It's probably not too great of a risk factor if you don't have it outside for more than a few minutes at a time, but it could still cause degradation.

If the sun is behind you, you'll have lots of shadows. It also results in "blowing out" (overexposing) the details that are visible in a softer, more even light. Yet another problem that will be minimized if you find a surface bathed with indirect light.

If there's any sort of mist or fog in the air that's contributing to an excess of moisture, wait until later. Moisture is the kryptonite of paper images. When in doubt, don't take your photo out!

As soon as you locate a satisfactory place to take a picture of your paper snapshot, my best advice is to try a few test photos. Thank goodness the process is so much easier now than it used to be in my youth. Film made us think carefully about exposing every single frame. After you've decided you're ready to expose, release the shutter then check the image you made with your camera by zooming in to check out the details. Examine each of the corners and in the center of the image as you view it on the camera/phone screen, including the areas that are in shadow. Compare it to your original image (you can use the "+" sign to zoom in on the viewer immediately after you've just captured them in your camera).

If you detect any blurriness you may have created by movement, try to find something solid on which to rest your hand so you can steady the camera or phone before your next attempt. Get inventive. Also be aware that the original image you're copying may itself be somewhat blurry, especially if it's a snapshot. That's OK. Just make sure that the copy photo you're creating isn't what's causing the blur.

Obviously you can try to use a tripod, but sometimes they're more trouble than they're worth in these situations. You're simply trying to grab a shot of one single image and practice finding shapes, patterns and signs in it. If, after you experiment with an image, you want to go more in depth with Snapshot Archeology, you'll find lots of ideas for building a make-shift copy stand on the Web. Take a look at my homemade copy stand—shown on the following page—and I'll explain how to photograph large photos that are behind glass. You can certainly use the following technique for small snapshots as well. It'll all depend on how involved you want to become or how much you want to explore the messages in your photos.

Or you can move to using a scanner. A scanner makes this part of the process much more manageable if the paper print you want to copy is 8 x 10 inches or less.

When you're satisfied with the copy you've made of your original image, move the data to your computer as you usually would from your media card. Make a folder to store all the files you'll create as you progress through the process of excavation and observation.

My homemade copy stand.

WHAT TO DO IF THE IMAGE YOU WANT
TO EXPLORE IS BEHIND GLASS?

If there's a large framed image you want to explore hanging on the wall—or even a small one—I have a method for working with them too. Sometimes there's no way to remove a photo from the framing material without ruining it. Often the image will be firmly ensconced behind glass. Again, your biggest problem will be trying to get a copy of the print without encountering the glare that will inevitably be created if you use a flash.

Scanning is out of the question as a solution, even if the framed print is small enough to fit on the bed because the mechanism that exposes it has a bright light projected toward the subject.

First of all, make sure the glass is as clear as it can be by cleaning it with a little bit of vinegar and water spritzed on a dust-free cloth. Make sure the glass is completely dry as well.

You'll want to find an area in your environment with diffuse or indirect light in which to photograph your image. You might be able to place it on the floor or on a table.

My set-up for copying large prints (whether they're under glass or not) is shown on the previous page. You can see I have two soft light boxes on stands for copy work along with an inexpensive tripod I can manipulate to point straight down so the camera is positioned between its two front legs.

I have to climb up onto a step-stool to actually take the shot. I generally set the controls to automatic and hold very still when I press down on the shutter button. This is "good enough for government work" as the old saying goes. And it's perfectly fine for our purposes at this level.

The lights are pointed toward the subject (the original image) from two sides and the particular type of material that's stretched over the bulbs inside the box serves to diffuse the light. In fact, the fabric is called "diffusion material." There are no shadows because the light is not coming from a single source. Here I'm showing that you can use this method to copy most sizes of your paper prints, as well as your prints under glass.

Shown below are two examples of a large photo, framed in glass, I placed on my dining room table. Diffused light is falling on it from two windows. In the example on the left, the light is naturally bluish because it's the "cooler" temperature of the daylight spectrum. The photo copy on the left is blurry because I didn't use anything to steady my camera. You can also see some reflections in the glass even though the light is indirect.

Notice what happens when I use a flash? The color and tonality of the example on the right look more like the original appears in reality. Obviously the copy on the right is unusable because of the reflective glare from the camera flash.

You might also notice the glass protecting your print has different qualities that cause problems for you when you're trying to photograph it. Some glass has ripples while others may not be completely transparent. Your copy image can come out distorted. Again, if you keep experimenting—since all it will cost you is a little time—you'll capture a copy of your original that'll be a relatively accurate representation. The best approach is to be inventive and curious. Just keep remembering that you need plenty of indirect, diffuse light and a steady camera.

On the following page, the top image shows a makeshift lighting situation. The light bulbs are two different color temperatures. The left one is yellow and the right one is blue. That's a common situation when you're looking all over the place in your house for two lamps to use as lights.

To add a little more complexity to the project, there is also a window to the left in this arrangement. The reason I like this particular illustration is that the bulb on the left is the lower temperature, the more yellow-orange of most interior lamps, while the one on the right is a daylight flo (florescent). And even though shadows have been created by the step-stool, there are no shadows on the framed photo I'm copying.

Below, the copy on the left was made with the two soft boxes lighting it. The one on the right was made using the funky, non-matching light sources. For your purposes in exploring your image, the lighter, slightly-off color of the copy on the right is acceptable.

One of the most valuable lessons I've learned through the years is to not wait for everything to be perfect before you start. Start somewhere, then learn to adjust from what you learn and from your "mistakes." After you capture a reasonably good copy of your photo, transfer your digital image to your computer.

The Alphabet Parade

MY SNAPSHOT ARCHEOLOGY READING
AND ANALYSIS OF *THE ALPHABET PARADE*

It's perfectly fine for you to feel sorry for my kids, and assorted other relatives who are used as the guinea pigs in my demonstrations. They've given me their permission, albeit not always without reservations.

That's particularly true in the snapshot I've chosen to show you the ways in which I work with paper prints by hand.

1. Curiosity

As I was flipping through old photos, I was immediately drawn to this image because I had an emotional tie to it. And he has a great big, red bow tie! I could tell right away that there's quite of bit of action going on here in the shapes, forms, symbols and colors. My curiosity was piqued! All the initial requirements for an interesting session were in place. Curiosity at its most basic level is just plain fun. Our brain is like a child who has a wonderful time discovering patterns. It revels in finding spooky faces leering out from the shadows of leaves on the ground and comical characters dancing in the clouds.

It possesses a mechanism called the Reticular Activating System (RAS) that's always checking out the stimuli in its environment. The RAS is like a radar in your head that's constantly searching for the appearance of your personal preferences and also for the aspects of life that repel you or could cause you harm. It's functioning at high speed when you decide as an example you're going to buy a new car. It begins the process of looking for a particular type of a vehicle. Almost magically, you begin to see that specific make and model you favor all over town when you'd only ever spotted a few of them before your decision to buy one. In the same way your curiosity, along with your RAS, will happily guide you to the first element you'll want to explore in your image.

My son B has grown up to be a smart, handsome, talented guy (OK, I'm exercising a bit of a mom's prerogative here) who's an aerial photographer/cinematographer, musician and pilot. Even with all his many accomplishments and abilities, the one thing that made him the most unhappy as a child was attending school. He was the original self-directed learner, devouring books and magazines far above his supposed reading level on subjects like atmospheric weather conditions, engineering and aerodynamics.

He particularly disliked being required to dress up for certain celebrations or school functions. On those days he would literally plead with me to let him to stay at home. Sometimes I did allow it because, even at his young age, I believed he should have a little control over his life. This particular day, when he was in kindergarten, I didn't relent.

In the snapshot with which I'll be working as an example, it's very apparent—by the look on his face and his drooping shoulders—that he lost the discussion. He was forced to be "Mr. V" in an alphabet parade. I determined, as the parent, that it wouldn't be fair to all the other "letters" who'd gone to so much trouble to dress up as alphabet characters for one of them to be missing from the troop. So I forced my 6 year old to go. Sure it was hard to do. Naturally, he was cute. Of course the whole family came out to watch the cavalcade, which included wagons, tricycles and all sorts of kid contraptions that had wheels on them. Clearly, none of that support was in the least bit comforting to B. He was miserable and no one has to conduct a Snapshot Archeology excavation to see that it's written all over his face.

2. Investigative skills

The original image is a 3½ x 5 inch paper print that was created in circa 1987. At that time in history, digital cameras were still at least a decade away from being available to the consumer market. From the "softness" (another word for blurriness) I see in the print quality, I think my father probably snapped the shutter on this image with his little, inexpensive, disposable camera. Both B's father and I had professional 35mm Nikons with better lenses so I can generally narrow the search down as to which family member took the shot by examining the softness of the print image. Many times it broadens the "bandwidth" of the messages you'll receive if you can determine whether you took the snapshot you're excavating or if somebody else captured it.

Before I began my in depth engagement with the image, I took the smaller print to a Walgreens so I could scan my original photo and get an enlargement. It's also possible to accomplish this step at home. You can scan your image (as we talked about earlier) and send the digital file to a brick and mortar building where you can pick it up later the same day. Or you can find an online photo merchant (such as snapfish.com or shutterfly.com) to enlarge your photo and send it back to you via the postal service. That avenue can take up to a week unless you pay rush charges.

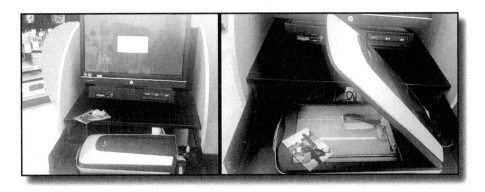

For now, let's get back to the way I approached this particular excavation. In the photos above, you can see Walgreen's store kiosk where I scanned the smaller, original image and then waited about 15 or 20 minutes for them to return an 8 x 10 inch enlargement to me. The cost was $4.31.

We're engaging in the analog/3-D form of what, later in the book, we'll be performing digitally to enable us to see the tiny clues hidden in our snapshots. We took a smaller paper image we'd scanned (or had transferred from our camera) and made it bigger. And the best thing is that our precious, little photo is still in its original, preserved state. Whatever we do to the enlargement is OK. Our historical, primary document is intact as long as we place it back into a storage situation that will ensure its safety.

The next thing I do, as I'm working with the enlargement, is to set up my light box. I have a couple of them, but the one I've come to prefer comes from a company who makes them, primarily, for tattoo artists. People frequently use these lighted surfaces to trace stencils. The price varies depending on the surface size you prefer. The larger the lighted area, the more expensive the light box.

I used to have a really big one for looking at hundreds of slides at once and now wish I hadn't gotten rid of it. But I gave it to the kid in the picture we're excavating to use so it seems like a fair trade at the moment. Anyway, I like the compactness of the one I use now because I usually work on 8 x 10 inch enlargements or smaller.

In order to accommodate the reality that the print I'm exploring is a vertical, I've adjusted the light box until it was turned 90 degrees from its first position so I could work on it more easily. You'll notice that, when you place a print on the light box, it appears brighter. It appears that way because it is.

The happy result of this is that you'll be able to decipher many more details than if you were attempting to trace the artifacts without the light box.

I place a small piece of double-sided tape on the top of the photo so that it secures it onto the light box along with the piece of translucent drawing paper I'll be laying over the top of the picture.

Now I have in front of me the equivalent of the analog/3-D version of layers in Photoshop.

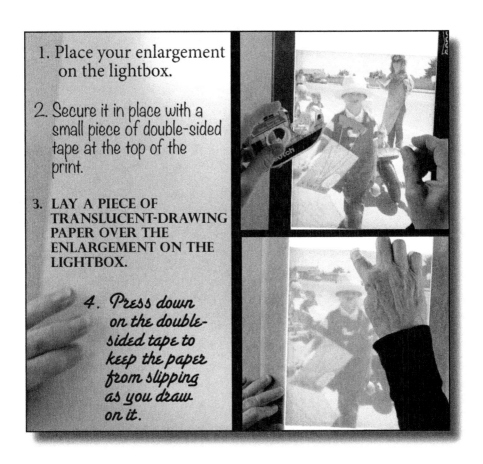

1. Place your enlargement on the lightbox.

2. Secure it in place with a small piece of double-sided tape at the top of the print.

3. LAY A PIECE OF TRANSLUCENT-DRAWING PAPER OVER THE ENLARGEMENT ON THE LIGHTBOX.

4. *Press down on the double-sided tape to keep the paper from slipping as you draw on it.*

3. The ability to identify an element that has the potential to yield interesting artifacts

In this step I'm referring to our capacity to discern some elements in our image that have the possibility of conveying a message to us. Some of these will be the first shapes or forms that caught our attention and encouraged us to choose one photo over another. The "V" shape repeats so often and so obviously in this snapshot of my son that it's the first "anchor" for me as I examine the image further.

I notice that a "V" has a point that's directional. I can see it repeated in several places on the image. The "V" itself on the poster board. The crook of the teacher's elbow. The V-shaped shadow just to the right of my son's knees that's being cast on the sidewalk. When I see repeating shapes, I know I've found compelling elements with which I can work.

As soon as I notice elements this clearly in a photo, I reach for a reference guide. I used to depend on several trusty books, along with the Internet, to figure out initial meanings. However, since I've been investigating my images for a while now, I've put together the guide included in this book.

4. Preliminary reference guide **for the identification of artifacts (symbols, patterns, colors, forms, numbers)**

I always have my copy of the Basic Symbols and Their Meanings on my worktable for reference. You can open this book up to the reference section on pages 79–99 to give you some visual examples to get started. Or you can download a PDF from www.ChristiKoelker.com/snapshot-archeology/ if you'd like to print it out.

Using this reference is a good way to get a look at how to divide and categorize the shapes, symbols and forms you notice. I have to admit that sometimes I'm not sure whether what I'm seeing is a form, a shape or a symbol.

Here's the rule-of-thumb I use: a symbol is a something that's a representation of something else. The bowtie, in the image I'm excavating, is the symbol for a real object in the world of things. It symbolizes something like the finishing touch on a gift. Or the manner in which a person wears a piece of cloth to dress up their clothing. Letters and numbers are symbols. Not the counting up of how many of somethings there are in a picture, but the actual letter or number itself.

A form or shape is a distinct object or outline of an external surface that "forms" a shape. Triangles, circles, squares or ovals are forms or shapes. They are, in themselves, "symbolic." They have meanings that are historically connected with them, but we'll label them as forms in Snapshot Archeology.

On the Reference Guides, I've used the word "symbol" to also describe a shape or form. It's a little confusing and it's also somewhat subjective. Certain people only understand an element when I call it whatever term that's familiar to them. This is a sticking point I've often encountered, but I've labeled shapes that particular way in the reference so, when we move on to the next step of analyzation, we'll be able to match the universal/historical meaning of a shape/form to a symbol.

In my listing of the elements I see in my image, I've called the geometric shapes I found in my photo "forms." But when I go to the reference section to see what each means, I'll look under the "symbol" section.

I hope that makes sense. The words will naturally become interchangeable after a few excavations. Try not to get stuck here on semantics. Just follow the visuals in the reference guide and you'll be fine.

Now I'll switch gears a bit to engage my analytical skills. I'll take each of the elements of the artifacts I've found and match them up using the reference guide.

5. Critical thinking to separate primary artifacts from the less informative ones

The very first detail in the image that draws my attention is the "V" formed by the teacher's elbow directly to the right of B's hat. She's either wearing a scarf around her neck that's blowing away from her or (what looks more likely to me) there's a beam of light shining between her and B. I'm more inclined towards this theory because I can see her arm through the artifact. This frequently occurs in photos, particularly in snapshots. Her attention is focused on B in the moment and so is her energy.

Not so very long ago I would try to explain away this phenomenon of light repeatedly showing up in snapshots as a figment of my imagination. Yet I've witnessed it over and over as I've examined thousands of images. It's become apparent to me that light uses the instant the shutter is clicked to interact within the scene.

6. Visual mapping of your artifacts

Next, I either get the Snapshot Archeology artifact checklist sheet, a journal/ notebook or just a plain piece of paper so I can record the elements I see as I discover them during the excavation process. This is an important step because you can easily lose your way once you step inside the image.

Documenting your finds immediately also helps you to refocus and reorient yourself during your "dig." Sometimes simply stopping to assess what you see by writing it down will lead you in a new direction of inquiry or point you toward an area of the image you hadn't noticed when you started.

You can download my Snapshot Archeology Artifact Checklist Sheet from www.ChristiKoelker.com/snapshot-archeology/.

7. Artifact documentation

I love to use color to mark the areas where compelling elements show up for me. As I said before, this hands-on approach is my favorite way to interact with my images. It's relaxing and, at the same time, it's creative. When I'm working on translucent/tracing paper, I first indicate the positions of the elements with a regular pencil. Later, after I've identified all the artifacts I find, I'll fill the areas in with colored pencils. If I'm using acetate—it's the very same process only using clear pages instead of translucent ones—I use permanent markers. Should you decide to use acetate pages, don't make the mistake of using white board markers because they rub off if you touch the sheet.

In the photo on the previous page, I've indicated what I've found in yellow so you can more easily see how I started. You'll notice how many "Vs" are surrounding Mr. Velvet Vest, B's character in the alphabet parade. The Vs are formed by the shape of his collar against his neck and a shadow beside the little girl on the (what we used to call in the 80s) "Big Wheel." Even the spoiler on the extended rear section of the Big Wheel can be seen behind B's right shoulder (from the viewer's perspective) with the inside design forming the only inverted V. To me, it seems to mirror his funny, yet sad, little mustache.

The overall feeling I get when I look at the snapshot now is one of playfulness. Certainly not in his physical demeanor, but everywhere else around him. It's as if the elements surrounding my stoic boy on that particular day are saying, "Cheer up little one because what's a smile but a frown turned upside down?" And what's a point-up V but a point-down V turned upside down? The recognition is solid for me. It reinforces what's occurred since that moment in our lives in that there's always support from the imperceptible universe around us. That's particularly been the case for my son. Some may call it a guardian angel or others a lucky star. He's been protected over and over by a force we can't see with our naked eyes as we go about our daily lives. Not much more than a year ago, those invisible guardians showed up to save his life in the midst of a devastating car accident. He described it to me as, "time slowing down" and as "feeling myself being pushed back away from the impact." When the progression of images slows down, like pressing "stop" on the TV remote. Then there it is!

The more you engage with your personal photographs, the more you'll experience this precise phenomenon.

Now, back to the excavation at hand. I've finished writing down all the Vs I've discovered on my data sheet (just like a working archeologist). I'm not going to decide whether or not I'll keep all of the artifacts I've found at this point because I haven't finished digging yet.

Keep	ID/Area on Image	Symbol	Form	Color	Number	Other
☐	upper middle right	V (point down)		N/A	1	made by the crook in the teacher's elbow
☐	center	V (point down)		N/A	1	seen at the neck of B's golf shirt
☐	center	V (point down)		N/A	1	created by the overlap of B's vest
☐	center left	V (point down)		green	1	the V drawn on the poster B's carrying
☐	to the right of B's elbow	V (points toward viewer)	triangle	silver/gray	1	on the front of the little girl's robe
☐	lower right	V (points toward viewer)		black	1	the shadow cast by the trike wheel
☐	center	V (point up)			1	Appears to be resting on B's right shoulder
☐						

ARTIFACTS FOUND IN IMAGE/SNAPSHOT B's Alphabet Parade 1987 DATE 10/18/2014

Let me reiterate here that I'm not trying to get you to agree with the feelings I'm having and connections I'm making with this very special and personal photograph of mine. Remember what I've been repeating since the beginning of the book? It's this aspect of the explanation process that's probably the most difficult part of Snapshot Archeology and image alchemy to express. You won't experience the same things I do because we're different individuals. I bring my 30-plus year history with my child to the excavation with me. I know the sequence of events that happened up until the recorded minute and for 20-some years hence. You can see the specific shapes and symbols I'm pointing out to you as an exercise to teach you how to find the artifacts in your own images. I'm also able to show you the elements and artifacts in your snapshots if you ask me to do so, but I can't interpret them on the deep level that I'm able to do with my own images. I'm simply giving you a map to reference, but you'll have to drive the actual "road" on your own.

I'm going to move on from the Vs in the snapshot (even though I've also found two more tiny white ones created by his golf shirt collars). I'll enter them on my data sheet during my next go-around. But for now I can see how tightly all the Vs are concentrated around B. That's curious! So I'll make a mental note of it. I could go ahead and write that observation down as a note on my paper so I won't forget. Remember, nobody will be grading your work. Add as many notes, arrows and reminders as you need to help you when you begin to put all the information together later for analyzation purposes. This is all about you and what you see.

Now, as I look again at the image, I'm drawn into investigating his hat, as well as the light and dark stripes in his shirt. Light and dark stripes denote contrast. When you get to the digital excavation, be sure to look at the family photograph and you'll see this same dashing fellow is wearing a cap with horizontal stripes. Contrary to his less than gleeful expression here, he's got a big smile on his face in that photo. The stripes in the hat he's wearing in the Christmas photo are not as far apart in values as the shirt he has on here many years earlier. He's chosen grey and blue stripes later in his life as opposed to the stark white and dark blue in this instance. That indicates to me that some of the same contrasting aspects of life are still there, but they've been much more integrated. A reality I know, as his mom, to be true. One aspect that piques my curiosity in the Christmas photo is the explanation as to why B's the only one wearing a hat and a coat when we were in the house. Now you'll have something to look for when we get there!

Contrasting horizontal lines can indicate conflicts or, in this case, the child facing the world as he begins to venture out into his bigger, unpredictable life. He much would've rather stayed at home to work on building model airplanes. Mechanically, he was far ahead of his classmates. He was a born engineer, sketching experimental flying vehicles from a very early age. But suddenly the familiar times, during which he was left to engage in the activities that helped his days make sense to him, were overlaid with the requirements forced upon him as he grew old enough to go to school.

We often laugh about that these days because B's daughter H absolutely loves school, along with all the related pageants, parties and parades. She's pictured on the following page with her mom just after she was wrapped up in toilet paper at a kindergarten Christmas party so she would look like a "snow girl." She's more than happy to pose and smile.

Isn't it interesting that we can compare these three events frozen in snapshots so many years apart? Almost all of the elements in the photo of H and her mom are roundish and easy going compared to the sharp angles in the one we're excavating of B's alphabet parade.

Look above H's left shoulder (from your orientation as the viewer). There's the same sort of playfulness in the appearances of shapes we see in B's image except that she's surrounded by lazy, soft circles and ovals. Closest to her shoulder is a green star. She's also wearing a hat. The image has a very feminine energy to it as compared to the pointed, angular, male energy of her father's kindergarten snapshot. My wonderful daughter-in-law beams. The "contrasts" and similarities between the two images are extraordinary. And one of the lovely surprises of Snapshot Archeology is that appearances such as these are more common than not.

I mentioned earlier in this section that I found two small, white triangles forming the collar of B's golf shirt. Those have been outlined in pencil along with the diagonal stripes in the shirt and his hat.

Keep	ID/Area on Image	Symbol	Form	Color	Number	Other
☐	upper middle right	V (point down)		N/A	1	made by the crook in the teacher's elbow
☐	center	V (point down)		N/A	1	seen at the neck of B's golf shirt
☐	center	V (point down)		N/A	1	created by the overlap of B's vest
☐	center left	V (point down)		green	1	the V drawn on the poster B's carrying
☐	to the right of B's elbow	V (points toward viewer)	triangle	silver/gray	1	on the front of the little girl's trike
☐	lower right	V (points toward viewer)		black	1	the shadow cast by the trike wheel
☐	center	V (point up)			1	Appears to be resting on B's right shoulder
☐	hat	arch	half-oval	straw	1	
☐	collar of shirt		triangles	white	2	framing his face
☐	stripes on shirt		horizontal lines	blue and white	4	stark contrasts
☐	hat brim			straw		looks like something to hide under
☐						
☐						

ARTIFACTS FOUND IN IMAGE/SNAPSHOT B's Alphabet Parade 1987 DATE 10/18/2014

The upward pointing V and the V created by his teacher's elbow are still shown in this view. The V on B's poster board and the V that appears to be resting on his shoulder almost seem to shelter him between them in a protective way. This view shows that relationship clearly. The V created by the overlap of his vest visually links the sheltering Vs. I'm going to add the new elements I've found to my list.

There's another shape that's calling to me in the image. I'm beginning to home in on ovals. Initially I notice, during this phase of excavation, that B is holding something in his hands. Certainly should have seen the maracas in the smaller, 3½ x 5 inch print, but I didn't!

An argument could be made by people—and I've engaged in this particular discussion often—that it's no big deal to notice something that's been printed on an image for many years.

Yet, over and over I've seen extraordinary connections manifest when we consciously witness the various forms, shapes, symbols, numbers and colors in our personal snapshots.

B is holding two maracas, one in each hand. Immediately my mind flashes on the fact that this image was captured long before he expressed his interest in percussion instruments and years before he played the drums. He's holding onto them a manner that appears to me, by his relaxed grip, that he's gaining a bit of comfort from them. The shape of a maraca looks like an oval on a stick. Or perhaps a little like a person's head on a neck. Remember, as strange as the previous analogy might seem, we're always looking for repeating patterns. It's not for us to necessarily make connections at this juncture, even though they'll pop into our minds unbidden.

As I ponder the other shapes in the image I see between the borders of my print, I recognize that the shape of the maracas shows up again as the teacher's oval head (I've indicated that in the last frame above as #1). And as soon as I dive into a specific shape, I find them all over the place as my RAS (Reticulating Activation System) kicks into high gear to search for the similar patterns.

I find it helps me to lift the translucent/tracing paper off of the light box every now and then so I can look at the new image that's taking shape.

Number 2, as indicated in the last frame of the collage above, is a repeating echo of the maraca B holds in his right hand. Because the sun is behind the subjects, this semi-circle is created not by the maraca but by the shadow from the trike wheel.

Below I've drawn a yellow line around the ovals I found in the image. I've also discovered another oval I didn't see at first. Look on B's "V" poster board. There's a smaller V printed inside a white oval. I'll add these to my list.

The last artifact I'm going to add to my checklist is the big, red bow that's situated itself in a diagonal slant on his chest. In a droll manner, it's in the center of the scene. It adds to the ambiance of surrender to the bigger forces (the grown-ups) who have orchestrated this event. It reminds me of a crooked smile on the face of a cartoon character after a trick has been played on him.

Keep	ID/Area on Image	Symbol	Form	Color	Number	Other
☐	upper middle right	✓ (point down)		N/A	1	made by the crook in the teacher's elbow
☐	center	✓ (point down)		N/A	1	seen at the neck of B's golf shirt
☐	center	✓ (point down)		N/A	1	created by the overlap of B's vest
☐	center left	✓ (point down)		green	1	the V drawn on the poster B's carrying
☐	to the right of B's elbow	✓ (points toward viewer)	triangle	silver/gray	1	on the front of the little girl's trike
☐	lower right	✓ (points toward viewer)		black	1	the shadow cast by the trike wheel
☐	center	✓ (point up)			1	Appears to be resting on B's right shoulder
☐	hat	arch	half-oval	straw	1	
☐	collar of shirt		triangles	white	2	framing his face
☐	stripes on shirt		horizontal lines	blue and white	4	stark contrasts
☐	hat brim			straw		looks like ~~something to~~
☐						hide under
☐	various areas		oval	various	12	
☐	center	bow		red	1	bow on a gift; to top it off
☐						
☐						

ARTIFACTS FOUND IN IMAGE/SNAPSHOT B's Alphabet Parade 1987 DATE 10/18/2014

8. Analytical skills *to interpret your excavated data*

I'm finally ready to take all of the various data I've collected up to this point in my Snapshot Archeology excavation and begin to interpret them as a whole.

I'll look back at my checklist to decide which artifacts I want to examine more closely and which ones I don't want to include during this current analysis.

There's only one artifact I'm going to ignore this time. It's the smaller, silver/gray, V/triangle on the nose of the little girl's trike. I might go back to it at later, but right now, it doesn't intrigue me enough to include it in my upcoming analysis.

As I return to the translucent/tissue paper to color in the areas I've outlined in pencil, I'll refer to my checklist to make sure I don't forget anything. While I'm filling in the areas, I also may discover another element I didn't notice earlier. In that case, I'll go back to the last two steps of visually mapping my image and documenting the artifacts I find on my checklist.

9. *Journal entries* to interpret your individually generated data

I suggested earlier that you find some sort of special journal, notebook or paper to begin writing down your interpretations. I use several different versions of journaling (or you might simply call it finding the meaning) depending on my level of interest in a "dig" or if I want to save it for a particular purpose. I've not settled on any one method as being better than any other. As a matter of fact, I'm relatively sure that you'll discover even more innovative ways to curate your excavations than I show here. For inspiration, visit the art supply store or browse the Internet for some of the fabulous creations of scrapbook and mixed media artists. Then please share new ideas on www.ChristiKoelker.com.

For the purposes of this exercise though, I've decided to put each of the pieces I'm working on and all of the other related things together into a photo album. Sometimes I like to save my Snapshot Archeology excavations and analyses in this fashion because it displays all the steps in the process I've gone through. Friends and family often want to understand how I've made the connections I talk about so saving the pieces together as a group helps me explain it to them visually. It also allows them to follow along with me as I point out what I noticed. It draws them into a conversation during which they make connections of their own.

Just a tiny discussion here about the colors you choose for filling in the outlines. I have a mid-range price set of 24 colored pencils. You don't have to buy the most expensive ones. Borrow them from your kids but hide the good set if you really get serious. I really want to splurge on something like these over-the-top, 300-(plus)-dollar beauties on the left in the photo below. Yet somehow I muddle through with my compact army of faithful sweeties on the right.

The Snapshot Archeology Journal page I'm going to use is shown below next to some other notebooks I have. If you want to download a PDF to print, visit www.ChristiKoelker.com/snapshot-archeology/.

Now, it's back to the light box for me as I decide how I want to fill in the outlined artifacts. I certainly could have colored in the elements from the enlargement three steps back as an extension of the visual mapping process but I enjoy including it along with the journaling phase. Especially when I'm working by hand. I find this part of the technique similar to the other crafts I pursue in my life (writing, photography or editing in filmmaking) in that, when I sink deeply into the activity without interruption, there's less of a hindrance in communication among my eyes, hands, brain and heart.

This stage is also an exciting and expectant time. I know from experience that I'll see more than when I traced the initial outlines in pencil. What will bubble up to the surface of the image? What will I remember? What was going on in the instant when I was standing with my father, and surely my mother too, that I missed?

I have no doubt it will be emotional because it nearly always involves feelings tinged with joy, sadness, longing, resentment, glee or some combination of any number of emotions. Both my parents have passed on now. Will I remember what they said in those moments as we watched the kid we all adored stoically march through an event he found humiliating? Of course, we chuckled at his discomfort because hadn't we all been in those situations before? Wasn't it some sort of American rite of passage in which we were involved? Didn't we have to make him participate in a school function so he would become a more responsible human being?

Those are the types of thoughts that are likely to float through my mind as I color in the outlines. As I literally and figuratively fill in the sketches of life as it was captured more than two decades ago, I'll challenge myself to face the messages waiting for me inside this vessel we call a snapshot of an "insignificant" burst of historical time that I would never have even considered with more than a brief glance. Not until I performed this measured, intentional, interactive excavation.

Sure enough. There they are. Right on schedule, the questions come.

The dots start to become connected.

I notice, as I color in the crook of the teacher's arm (the first entry on my checklist) that she's holding something in her hand. It may be a microphone or something that echoes the maracas in B's hands. That's interesting. Also something that happens often when I begin coloring in the outlines. I'll note this below the last entry on my checklist and go back as I work my way down the page.

	areas		oval	various	12	
✓	center	bow		red	1	bow on a gift; to top it off
o	upper and center		oval	dark	1	teacher holding something
▢						
▢						

I denote my new find with an "o" instead of a check mark so I'll remember that I discovered this new artifact when I was coloring in the pencil outline after my first pass through.

I've identified the "beam" of light I found earlier, but didn't write down the first time through, by a dotted line. In the close up detail, it's evident that her arm is seen through it. It may be lens flare. I'm not claiming it's paranormal but even if I did express the phenomenon in those terms, paranormal actually means something that occurs "para" or alongside something else that's considered by science as "normal." It's an anomaly that can't be quickly explained away. Rarely will any of us have the opportunity for our personal photographs to be examined by a team of scientists. In books and blogs to come, I'll go more in depth about the many intelligences possessed by light.

In this instance, and in the ways you'll be reading your photographs, simply notice where a light shows up within your scene. Many times you'll be surprised and, speaking for myself, humbled by the ways we ignore the very energy that supports life on earth. We don't consciously consider the multitudes of ways it surrounds and sustains us in every moment of our lives. If for no other reason, noticing the particular places light shows up in images to dance with us, in us and around the surfaces of our photographs opens up an extraordinary channel of appreciation with a dynamic force of the cosmos. It's with this first element that I decide I want to start making notes on my journal page.

Under the "Observations" section of my journal page I quickly, in one or two lines, jot down my mental remarks for the first time in a written form. Then under "Notes" I write down that I'm not certain of the source of the light and perhaps the teacher is wearing a scarf or tie of some sort around her neck.

I'll put another line through the check beside the artifact I've just finished exploring.

Keep	ID/Area on Image	Symbol	Form	Color	Number	Other
✗	upper middle right	✓ (point down)		N/A	1	made by the crook in the teacher's elbow
✗	center	✓ (point down)		N/A	1	seen at the neck of B's golf shirt
✗	center	✓ (point down)		N/A	1	created by the overlap of B's vest
✓	center left	✓ (point down)		green	1	the V drawn on the poster B's carrying
	to the right of B's elbow	✓ (points toward viewer)	triangle	silver/gray	1	on the front of the little girl's smile

ARTIFACTS FOUND IN IMAGE/SNAPSHOT _B's Alphabet Parade 1987_ DATE _10/18/2014_

Looking down the column of my list, I glance at the V formed by the collar of B's golf shirt and the repeating V beneath it where his vest buttons together. Neither of these artifacts are particularly exciting at the moment. I apply the line to the check on my list to show I've looked at them during this step and move on.

The next area I decide to focus on is the poster board that B is carrying. When I looked really closely at it, I realized that there are actually three different shades of green on it.

The pencils' tips indicate the variations of green I used on the area in which I applied them. The big "V" is the lightest of the three with almost a green apple hue. The upper side of the background has the sun shining on it and so it's lighter than the darker green cutting diagonally across the bottom area. I used the darkest shade of green there because that section is in the "shade." I left the white oval behind the second "V" alone. I'll come back to that location in just a bit to reveal a surprise. In the mean time, are you noticing how the words we use denote the amount of light we see? Shade refers to the shadow portion of the poster board and also refers to the intensity of the colored pencil.

Simply by adjusting the pressure on your pencil, you can create all shades of colors. Mix them (apply one over another) to produce different hues.

Now turn your attention to the last frame of the three images above where the red pencil tip is pointing toward the top edge of the green poster board.

This is just one of the two surprises that popped out for me on this crazy V-letter poster as I was coloring the various areas of it. There they are! Two red "Vs" formed by the red yarn or string that was holding B's poster board around his neck. This is where I ask myself, why "Vs"? Why aren't the ends tied in a bow? B has on a red bow, so that would have been an echo artifact. But no, it's two Vs and they're pointed up, directed at my little man. I add this find to my artifact sheet and mark it with an "o."

Then I start to work on sketching around the edges of something that caught my eye earlier in the white oval on the green poster board. Look who shows up.

Keep in mind that I've been working on this image for quite a few days now as I move through each part and document it for the purposes of relating the process in this book. In all that time I never saw this little fellow hiding in plain sight!

It's a mini-B! Complete with the big brim on his hat and his vest. I know, in the days prior to the alphabet event, we tried to find the right clothing to depict the character B was portraying, but seeing this badge-like effigy that my little boy is carrying around his neck certainly sets my mind reeling.

Needless to say I also add this to the artifact checklist, mark it with an "o" and move on before I get too sucked into what's beginning to feel a little uncomfortable to me.

	areas		oval	red area	1	bow on a gift, to top it off
✓	center	bow		red	1	
o	upper mid center		oval	dark	1	teacher holding something
o	on the top of the poster bd	V		red	2	why are they V's?
o	in white oval on poster		drawing of small man		1	did we copy the drawing?

I'm actively refusing to allow myself to get bogged down here even though there's a powerful energy in the image. The fact is that I don't know how it will play out when I connect all the other artifacts together. An archeologist doesn't make assumptions by digging up just one compelling artifact out of the ground. He or she must put all of the pieces together before making inferences.

So back to my image and the light box. I've already decided I don't want to look further at the little silver triangle on the girl's trike. The next area I indicated I wanted to look at was the shadow cast by her trike. I can't really tell if it's her pedal or a combination shadow from her pedal, her foot and some angle of the sun being blocked by them together. I'll just take a pencil with a dark color and fill it in, watching expectantly for something else to appear as I scribble away in and around the lines I sketched earlier.

This detail offers us a good time to talk about the freedom we all have in interpreting the artifacts we find in our personal images. While I noticed the uneven area to the far right on the image (shown under the translucent/tracing paper) I didn't copy it exactly as I was filling in the shape. I see a repeating V in this general shape. Another viewer might see something else altogether.

All this to say that what really matters is that you understand that it's your image. If you recognize a symbol, form or shape that's meaningful for you and piques your curiosity then stick with your own guidance (G.U.T.) system. It matters very much in the final step that you're true to your intuition.

My feelings are that this is an unusual place for a dark V to show up in the snapshot. Yet it gives me a new certainty that the sun was high in the New Mexico sky at that time of the day and is providing me with a new influx of information that anchors my physical body to the snapshot between late morning and early afternoon. From this data, I realize for the first time that B is wearing a short sleeve shirt. So is his teacher. In fact, even though I've already focused on seeing her bare arm through the light beam, it's not until this moment that I recognize the fact. The temperature must have been warm that day. I can feel that warmth right now as I become aware of these clues that I never took the time to notice before. With that realization, a torrent of associations flood my mind.

Again, I acknowledge them but look back to my checklist so I can stay in this moment while at the same time observing the multi-dimensionality of the image beginning to rise up to meet me. For me, it's the connection to the weather that day that's become the catalyst and unlocked the deep magic of the image.

Now I have to try to keep my excitement at bay while I move through the rest of the artifacts I've recorded on my artifact checklist.

I move between looking at the image I'm filling in with my colored pencils on the light box, my artifact checklist and my Snapshot Archeology pages. As usual in this part of the process, many more messages begin surfacing. My mind races to start connecting all the "dots" I see appearing.

This is sort of like when I go shopping without a list and I start to put items in my basket without filtering out whether I really need or want them. I can certainly buy them, but I'm just going to set them in the basket so I can roll them around with me a while until I discern if they'll add value to my life. You'll see aspects of your image that literally pop out at you and almost shout, "Look at me! I'm important!" Each of those elements may well be. You can add them to the bottom of your list. However, it's better if you keep yourself grounded by using the checklist to guide you, so you don't jump to conclusions too soon.

This is the most exciting part! We've arrived at the place where the snapshot has opened up to us. It's ready to communicate because we've done the digging. We've demonstrated our purposeful intention. I could explain it further but I want you to experience it in your own way without me defining what it feels like to me anymore than I already have done.

On the following page are two of my completed worksheets. You can see the way in which I've consulted my artifact checklist first and then written down my observations on my journal page.

As I've filled in the outlines with colors, I've discovered some elements that help reinforce my decision to excavate this particular image. I'm going to remove my finished piece from the light box and place it in the album. Then I'm going to get a cup of tea to allow myself some time to absorb the new image that's appeared in front of me. It's the map I've created from the artifacts I've found within the snapshot.

Keep	ID/Area on Image	Symbol	Form	Color	Number	Other
✗	upper middle right	V (point down)		N/A	1	made by the crook in the teacher's elbow
✗	center	V (point down)		N/A	1	seen at the neck of B's golf shirt
✗	center	V (point down)		N/A	1	created by the overlap of B's vest
✗	center left	V (point down)		green	1	the V drawn on the poster B's carrying
✗	to the right of B's elbow	V (points toward viewer)	triangle	silver/gray	1	on the front of the little girl's trike
✗	lower right	V (points toward viewer)		black	1	the shadow cast by the trike wheel
✗	center	V (point up)			1	appears to be resting on B's right shoulder
✗	hat	arch	half-oval	straw	1	framing his face
✗	collar of shirt		triangles	white	2	
✗	stripes on shirt		horizontal lines	blue and white	4	stark contrasts
✗	hat brim			straw		looks like something to hide under
✗	various areas		oval	various	12	
✗	center	bow		red	1	bow on a gift; to top it off
✎	upper and center		oval	dark	1	teacher holding something
✎	on the top of the poster B's in white	V		red	2	why are they Vs
✎	oval on poster		drawing of small man		1	did we copy the drawing?
✎	teacher's on apron		triangle	dark gn	1	super teacher emblem :)
✎	on girl's trike		triangle & portions	red	3	3 red forms create triangle

---

Snapshot Archeology Journal

Date	Image	Observations	Notes
10/18/2014	B's Alphabet Parade 1987 "light from teacher"	B's teacher is looking at him with such caring on her face. The "beam of light" that seems to be sent out from her towards him shows me that she was supporting him on a deep level. I see she knows this is difficult for him.	I'm not sure if it's actually light or if the teacher has on a tie of some sort.
	Vs at the neck of B's shirt; where his vest comes together; shadow of trike wheel and over his right shoulder.	V, to me, could represent a downward pointing arrow. That would make sense as pointing down could mean "down" as in depressed. B was very unhappy. His personal energy was "down". The small triangle/V resting on his right shoulder is point up.	Reminds me of the idea of a devil sitting on one shoulder & an angel sitting on the other. Up point is the heavens. Encouragement, support, love. His teacher is beaming it to him. I know his family was sending happy thoughts as well.
	B's hat	It's a hat made out of a natural product. Straw. It's also very large & rests very big on his little boy head. The brim reminds me of representing everybody who came to see him dress up to be in the parade.	Arches are built to walk under & through to go from inside to outside or vice versa. If it were large enough, a person could keep from getting wet or stay out of the sun. If it had an overhang, a person would be even more protected. That's the function of the hat in this image. B's able to find some relief from the embarrassment underneath it.
	2 little, white triangles under his shirt collar formed by his shirt collar	This was part of his school uniform. The kids had to wear plain golf shirts (or they used to call them Polo shirts) because there was gang activity that occurred as a result of logos on shirts. In kindergarten? I think that now & I also thought it then.	This reminds me of angel wings.
	horizontal lines on B's shirt	Initially I thought the lines were more contrasting, but as I filled them in, I found they were more gray than white.	Horizontal lines represent places where the sky meets the earth. Nothing is a more horizontal landscape than New Mexico. It stands for stability, as do triangles. So even though B is having a hard time being present for this event, there is an overall tranquility infused into it. The contrast of the stripes certainly reinforces his conflicted feelings about the parade.

And just like every other archeologist I've ever seen work in the field, it's not until they finally get the map and the artifacts back to their lab that they can begin to truly analyze the things they've dug up. It's only then, with a fair amount of reflection, that they can write a really connected, cohesive record of their conclusions.

10. Conclusions **based on the combination of your excavated and individual data**

In this final step, we're going to move through putting all of the parts together in a "report" or, more casually, a story. We could use our cell phone apps to record our observations instead of write them down, but I think you'll find writing engages the tactile and the cerebral in a way that's rewarding.

I not only look at the image but I also listen to it. I allow it to "tell" me what the elements and artifacts I've discovered "say" all together. Keep in mind, as I've stressed before, the story I see and hear is for me alone. For purposes of explaining the process, I'll share some of them with you.

However, there's no possible way for you to be able to completely feel the heights and depths of revelation my image analysis will yield for me. Exactly in the same way I couldn't understand yours.

The image and sketch preserved in my album.

The finished sketch of *The Alphabet Parade*.
(Compare with the original snapshot on page 124.)

My Snapshot Archeology Analysis of
The Alphabet Parade

In the foreground of the image is a child who appears trapped in some alien place that has customs, clothing and festivities that are nonsensical to him. A breeze appears to blow through the snapshot from right to left, pushing aside not only his green poster board emblazoned with a large "V" but also the costume of the leader, behind him, who encourages B to participate in this peculiar rite of kindergarten passage. It's as if he's gotten off of whatever vehicle he was pedaling or pushing along the way to lodge a complaint. Or at least an acknowledgement. Why are all the other children but him on trikes and in wagons?

The small image of a cartoon "V" man inside the white oval on B's poster board B appears to be the blueprint for who he's meant to be in this scene. But the child doesn't want to be this little man. That's obvious. Even his clothes hang on him in dissent. They're too large for him. And so is his hat. Although that seems to be the only shelter for him anywhere in the photo.

The beam of light I initially found radiating from B's teacher emanates from a shield-like triangular area that appeared when I colored in her apron (or maybe it's a piece of fabric). When illuminated by the light box, this area is also a deeper shade of green. In her hand she holds a microphone or some object that looks to me now like a wand or a scepter. Her eyes, directed towards B, have been shaped by the lens of her sunglasses to reveal themselves as areas of darkness. I continue to get a very upbeat and supportive impression of her. Yet this addition of what looks like goggles dehumanizes her to some extent. Suddenly I realize that all the eyes in this photo are dark (because the sun is behind them of course). None of the children seem to have the spark of life one would hope to see in an activity such as this one.

V is an abbreviation for "versus." Here it's possibly B versus school life. In fact, that was so much the case for B and his relationship to school that this realization reaches into my consciousness in a profound manner. His teacher is trying diligently to encourage him to "march" or "roll" along with his classmates. However, he was having none of it and his expression of dejection is not only written all over his face but it's also captured in the elements that surround him in the scene.

The color green represents money, at least in the U.S. where this photo was taken. Could the intent underlying the tableau be, "Dress up like a man and go to school so you can learn enough to make money?" Then it may feel like "something hanging around your neck" or a "ball and chain" (notice the shadow beside his right hand) you'll carry around with you. But you'll be part of the crowd because everybody's rolling along with the parade.

This is as far as I'm going to go in explaining the connections I make in the snapshot we've been excavating together. Once again, I'm stunned by the language of the imagery. It always, always surprises me in the conclusion stage. I could go on for another page or so. I could even use the connections I see as a writing prompt to journal more in depth about it.

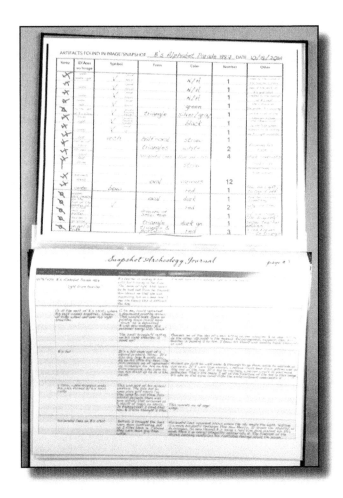

The album is where I'll store the final product. I'll keep my artifact sheets and journal entries in the clear pages located in the album after my sketch and conclusion. I might show it to friends and family or then again, I might keep it private.

There are certainly many more expansively creative ways in which you can display your Snapshot Archeology excavations. Please share your brilliant ideas and art pieces on the website at www.ChristiKoelker.com.

EXCAVATING YOUR PHOTOS DIGITALLY

I'll have to apologize here to readers who are working on PCs because I've used a Mac for over a decade now. The techniques I'm demonstrating in this chapter will transfer and relate to anyone who uses their computer to analyze their images. I may describe methods for moving images around that aren't exactly like the ones you find on either your laptop or desktop. However, when I've showed this method of identifying specific image artifacts to people during my workshops, they don't seem to have too many questions even if their equipment isn't the same as mine. Once again, it's OK to be inventive and curious. Your paper image is a digital one now so you don't have to worry that you'll mess it up.

We're ready to start digging in!

The image editing software I use is Photoshop. When I'm doing a Snapshot Archeology analysis, I don't actually change the exposure or any other feature of the image within the software as I might if I'm going to print a photograph for another purpose. I work within the program specifically so I can outline the features of the artifacts I find on "layers." Layers are the digital equivalent of sheets of transparent acetate (better than the semi-transparence of tissue paper). They can be virtually added "over" the original image (digitally represented within your software on your computer screen). You can add as many layers as you like. In my research, this particular feature seems to be a primary workflow on most image editing programs on the market. You can take it as far as you like and make it as complicated as you want.

I prefer to keep it simple though. In my experience, the snapshots can have so many shapes and forms going on that representing parts of them in a simple way helps me to see the messages more easily. I like to keep all my outlines on one layer so I can look at them as they relate to one another. However, sometimes I see distinct relationships between the shapes when I look at them apart from their original image. Every image is a different experience.

I have two different computers (a 2009 desktop and a 2014 MacBook Pro). I use both of them frequently but they have specific programs on them with various applications for video editing, writing or photography. For this demonstration,

I used the desktop. It has the older versions of both the Apple and the Adobe software. But as I said, I like to keep it simple as not that much has changed or been improved in the last five years as it relates to my analysis process.

iPhoto has often been the easy way for me to begin to search for a photograph I might want to analyze with Snapshot Archeology. I start the hunt by looking in my iPhoto Library. Apple introduced a more powerful app, Photos, in 2015.

iPhoto Library. The new Mac Photos app looks similar but is more complex.

Lately, I back up the photographs and snaps I collect on my phone by uploading them to an incredible service that I pay $99 a year to use. It's called Dropbox. (I used to use the software that Apple provided when my computer was purchased. I've filled up many a hard drive with the images I've transferred from iPhoto.) Now I have access to all my photos across all of my devices. I'll run across an image I can't wait to excavate by casually searching through it. It ignites the excitement of engaging in those first three steps I explained back in Part Two relating to curiosity, investigative skills and the ability to identify the "site" that has potential to yield interesting artifacts no matter where you digitally store your images.

Dropbox (Carousel is the organizing photo application associated with it)

In any case, whether you went through the process of transferring one of your paper prints to a digital form or you started with a digital file, we're ready to begin.

Step One: Attention and Intention are Critical for Opening the Doors to the Messages in Your Photos

After I pull my image up in Photoshop, I take a few moments to really engage with the image. In a very real sense, I meditate on it. I become totally focused and present before I dive into the picture. The attention and intention you bring to your analysis session will determine how much the image opens up to you. Try to keep in mind that you're not solely in the world of words anymore. Although words and sounds may float through your mind, you're in the embrace of a visual experience—one that may hold a great deal of energy and power in your life. Slip into it with the faith that what will emerge is something that will enhance your life. The messages you'll discover are parts of the missing pieces of a puzzle you've been trying to put together for years.

Try not to judge them or push them away. You can write down these impressions as they come to you. I've discovered that it sometimes helps to disconnect for a moment to process the journey in little bits. Your GUT Gauge will, in turn, interpret the symbols as you find them in your first language. Go as far as you can into the experience without overwhelming your mind and body. Look at the image. Take a little in. Allow it to settle. Return to look at the image deeper.

When you come closer to understanding even a portion of the message your image is transmitting, you'll begin to feel a type of a warmth start. It's very much like in the hide-and-seek game you may have played as a child when the person who's hidden something guides you by saying, "You're getting warmer…no, you're getting cooler." Perhaps you won't experience the warmth as a physical sensation of heat, but one of a feeling of recognition akin to the way you feel the warmth of an old friend when you meet him or her after many years. It's a recognition, a recollection, a remembrance. On a very deep level of cognition. Warmth is my term to describe the physical sensation I feel. At times I even get warm enough to take off a sweater in the winter or turn on a fan in the summer.

Just connect with the fact that you're honoring the way in which your Spirit perceives this life being spoken inside of you in language as old as you are today. Shifting to this particular style of interior communication takes practice and patience. When it finally happens, full-blown, you may see it all at once like a flash of lightening. You may be a little taken aback at the boldness (and almost giddiness) with which your intuitive voice responds to you once it realizes you've opened the door for it to contribute to your conscious world. It can act like the proverbial "kid in a candy store." You've unleashed it from its cave. It wants to comment on everything. You'll adapt rather quickly and learn how to rein it in so it can advise you as an intimate friend.

But now, we're just at the beginning of the process to open that portal to the part of ourselves that really understands we've been on exactly the right path all along. We see it documented in our photographs, snapshots and images of all kinds.

There's no "right" or "wrong" way to approach Snapshot Archeology. It really is all about you. The more you trust that what's inside you can be brought through the canal, so to speak, and visually expressed into an outer world through your images, the more you'll be childlike in the process. "Childlike" translates into being open to the wonder and magic of both the inner and outer spaces we've previously inhabited or presently inhabit.

Your Spirit is what animates you. It doesn't know religion or culture or boundaries. It only knows that it's eternal, boundless and fearless. Our quest now is to let our Spirits have the chance they've been patiently waiting for, to engage in flowing expression for a change. Unedited. Unjudged. You don't have to take responsibility for what your Spirit wants to express. You can just observe and listen. You don't have to take the result to an art critic review or show it to anyone else. You don't have to have Time-Life Books publish it and you don't have to hang it on the walls of the Metropolitan Museum of Art. It's yours and whoever you choose to share it with. The only promise I can make to you is that you'll know the answers to the subterranean questions that you've never quite asked out loud. I love that aspect about Snapshot Archeology. I love knowing that there are private aspects of myself that make sense, if only to me. It's enough. It's quite enough.

Like an archeologist, you dig up an artifact. You consider it within the context of the site you're excavating. You run it through your database of information about yourself and you comprehend a long-buried sign. A clue you left for yourself, and photographed, to someday lead you back home. That someday is now.

Step Two: Outlining Shapes, Forms, Numbers and Colors in Image Editing Software

I'm going to use this family photo I transferred to a digital form earlier in the book to demonstrate how to apply Snapshot Archeology to a digital image.

You can see me go through the process of excavating this image on my website.

I chose a picture of my own kids and grandkids taken on a happy Christmas holiday vacation several years ago to demonstrate to you that almost any photo can be filled with messages. I've never analyzed this particular image until I was preparing this section. It's a photo that's extremely precious to me. Even now, just thinking about the occasion on which it was captured makes me smile. In fact,

I have it framed and it hangs on a wall in my office. So I see it every day and am reminded of the people who are the most dear to me in all of the world. Yet, because I've never intentionally engaged with it before, it's never "opened" up to me. All that's about to change. Of course, there's a lot of positive energy inside this image for me because it was the first year both my children and their spouses had their schedules coordinate in such a way that we could be together with all their children on Christmas Day.

It was the first Christmas after both of my beloved parents (my kids' grandparents) had suddenly died within a brief two months of each other. It's safe to say that I adore this particular photograph. I can still recall the silliness and the lightness of our hearts as we teased each other until we had tears of laughter streaming down our faces. At some point we finally agreed that this would be a perfect time to go ahead and attempt a family photo.

Time out here.

Anybody who's ever taken on the challenge of getting lots of people who are related to collaborate on something as settled as a family photo on a holiday knows that it can quickly go south, especially if there are little ones involved. I was a bit nervous that it would add some stress to a lovely day.

The lake house where we were staying in Austin, Texas, had as its main holiday decorations more assorted flavors of large wooden nutcrackers (soldiers, bakers, kings, magicians) than any of us had ever seen assembled in one location. I don't recall today exactly who had the brilliant idea that each of us should choose the one nutcracker that appealed to us the most, but I think, as I revisit the photo that each of the adults in the picture take credit for it. It's certainly not a perfect portrait of our family. It's just a funny, documentary snapshot.

My son, the fellow that's all grown up from our last in-depth excavation, is in the striped hat. He placed his camera on a coffee table facing our crowd of giggly humans and set it to expose on a ten second delay. We chimped for about five shots all together and none of them turned out to be a staged, "professional" looking image. That's one of the elements I love most about it.

The version of Photoshop I use the most often is not latest version. I'm bringing that fact to your attention because you don't have to work on any really fancy software to do Snapshot Archeology on your images. When I do image alchemy readings of photographs and artwork for clients, I also use a drawing tablet with a dedicated stylus, but that's only so I can control the drawing better. When they receive their recorded video of the real-time analysis, the lines look straight and the circles look round.

After I prepare myself to be intentionally attentive I start to isolate the first shapes I've noticed. In Photoshop (PS), I make a duplicate layer so I can draw outlines of the elements I see (either with the line tool or with the brush tool). When I identify the first shape, it helps to anchor me inside the picture. As I explained earlier, it reminds me of standing on the edge of a pond that's rippling away as a soft breeze blows across the surface of it. I can make out a few murky formations that interest me way down on the bottom of the pond, but I can't yet see them clearly. So I metaphorically dive off into the water and I swim (direct my attention) toward finding one bold shape as a starting point. It's most likely to be a circle, a square, a triangle or an oval. Those are the most common and easy to find. When I locate one of them, I trace the outline of it with one of the PS tools I mentioned earlier. From the "home base" of that primary shape, I start looking around at the rest of the elements in the image.

As I'm in the process of identifying shapes, I don't try to make any sense of them at that point. I just find them and outline them. Usually I draw the outlining in a bright color. I keep merging the layers down as I go along, especially if I'm using a line tool, so there's not a hundred layers piled up on top of each other.

Here's an example of one of my personal Snapshot Archeology readings. This is more complex than what I do for clients but it works for me when I'm doing my own excavations.

I'm going to show you how I analyze this family snapshot from my own collection using the ten steps I originally introduced on page 57, but since we went through them so extensively in the previous paper excavation, I'm going to show you how to streamline them to go a little faster.

To recap, the basic steps are:

1. Curiosity

2. Investigative skills

3. The ability to identify some element that has the potential to yield interesting artifacts

4. A preliminary reference guide for the identification of artifacts (symbols, patterns, colors, forms, numbers)such as the Reference Guides provided in this book beginning on page 79

5. Critical thinking to separate the primary artifacts from the less informative ones

6. Visual mapping of your artifacts

7. Artifact documentation

8. Analytical skills to interpret your excavated data

9. Journal entries to interpret your individually generated data

10. Conclusions based on the combination of your excavated and individual data

The first step is *curiosity*. In some measure, you've already begun this preliminary process. I asked you to start off this digital session by focusing both your intention and attention on your image. As you were purposefully engaging with your image, your curiosity was naturally aroused. You noticed some element in the photo that you'd never seen before. I know this is the case because I've examined thousands of images. Every time I do a reading or am asked to help people excavate their snapshots they say, essentially, the same thing: "I've looked at this picture a hundred times," (or a thousand or a million) "and I never noticed that (shape, symbol, pattern, color, number) there before!"

The reason that's always the case is because the image doesn't reveal certain visual aspects of itself to you until you engage with it. Call it what you will. Define the reason that works best for you. All I can offer is the truth of what I observe each time I intentionally look at an image or guide someone else to do so. Certain elements will unveil themselves. The observer will recognize those elements as meaningful within the context of their individual life experience.

The difficulty for me, as always, is to try to find the words to "tell" you what you'll see. It's not possible for me to accomplish that feat. I can certainly give you tools and guideposts to find shapes, form, symbols and elements like them in your images, but I'd have to be you instead of me to explain what your interior cascade of data is constructing from all your visual, emotional and historical input. Only you can figure out what the elements in combination represent to you.

———

The aspect that I'm most curious about in the family snapshot I'm excavating here is the white, triangular light on the wall close to my granddaughter's head. The big, green arrow is pointing at the white area that's in the shape of a lopsided isosceles triangle.

I'm going to use the white triangle as my anchor point. If I use the "diving into the pool" metaphor, this is the shape I'll swim back to as I become more magnetized by the other elements of my photo.

As I look around from the vantage point of the white triangle, I'm interested in the bottom of the picture frame that's in the top, center of the image. You can see there's a bit of light shining on the glass, but what I think is more magnetic to me are the two edges that form black triangles.

When I see repeating elements, particularly formed by seemingly unrelated objects, it rivets my attention. I'm utilizing my investigative skills (step 2) to move around in the image with my eyes, and I'm engaging my ability to identify some element that has the potential to yield interesting artifacts (step 3).

You can see by the lines I've added to indicate the edges of the picture frame shaped like an arrow (directional angle) in green.

Even after looking at this snapshot for more than two years, my curiosity is piqued and something else is revealed. The three adult women in the family also are seated in a triangular formation. The coordinates of the three points are mapped by the oval shapes of our heads.

The placement of the family members in the photograph was unplanned.

Each person chose his or her own position on the couch or the floor. Actually, the two tallest people in the group are seated on the front row instead of in the back as I would usually place subjects in a group picture.

Initially, because of the intimate dynamics of my family, the three women being connected in such a striking way fills me with happiness. Each of us has a very different personality.

Yet, as I look at it and consider it briefly, I understand a deeper significance that was not in my consciousness before. Immediately, my heart is touched on an entirely new level. Yet for me to explain it to someone else would mean I would have to delve into extremely personal commentary that would take hours. Even if I wanted to try and publicly define the correlations, it wouldn't make sense to anyone else. Also, I have to keep myself from skipping ahead and move on. I'll save the analysis for later in the process.

I'll evaluate just two more elements in this image and then I'll continue with the next phase of the Snapshot Archeology process.

In the photo on the previous page, the green circle on the right is isolating the symbol of an anchor on the hat of the nutcracker held by my oldest grandson. Keep in mind that at this point I'm still looking (swimming) around to tag the elements that engage my curiosity. Even though I'm not analyzing yet, I make a mental note that he's a little bit hidden in the photo. It's a little surprising to me (and I've noticed it before of course) because he's definitely not a shy individual. He's actually extremely outgoing and people often comment on his confidence in the company of adults or in situations that might be uncomfortable to the majority of teens. That's just an observation to come back to and think about later.

On the left in the same photo is his younger brother, the middle son in a family with three boys. He's the only one who's chosen a Christmas character that's not a nutcracker.

He's chosen a Santa, which to me is a bit more conservative and traditional. Those are two accurate descriptors I'd use to describe my wonderful middle grandson's personality.

The last element to which I'm immediately drawn is the nutcracker held by my youngest grandson. (See detail below.) He's seated next to me in the photo and he holds what looks like a soldier nutcracker.

Just imagine being eight years younger than the next oldest in the family ahead of you and 10 years younger than the oldest. Might you have to know how to stand up for yourself? Certainly.

Also his nutcracker is the only one among the group that has its mouth open. This element has the potential to yield interesting aspects and so I circle this selection too.

Here's the entire snapshot with the elements we've identified indicated in green. I've added white boxes (step 6: visual mapping) next to the areas I think will offer me some valuable data. I'm not going to rule out any of these areas this time, as I might in some other situations. I'm keeping it relatively simple for our first digital image exploration.

When it comes time for you excavate your own photos, you might find yourself tagging lots of potential areas for analyses. It's at that point when you'll find Step 5 (critical-thinking to separate the primary artifacts from the less informative ones) will serve to keep you focused on the most relevant information.

You've probably already noticed that the Snapshot Archeology steps are not always in a set order. I've assigned a list with numbers so we can keep track of the individual techniques we'll use to analyze our images.

My Snapshot Archeology Analysis
of my Christmas Family Snapshot

Keep	ID/Area on Image	Symbol	Form	Color	Number	Other
✓	upper right		triangle	white	1	Made out of light
✓	top middle left & right		triangles	black	2	Corners of frame form 2 arrows
✓	multiple		ovals		3	Together the 3 ovals form a triangle
✓	middle right	anchor		gold	1	The anchor is stiched onto a hat
✓	middle left	Santa Claus			1	J. C. chose instead of a nutcracker
✓	upper middle left	soldier		gold	1	2. chose; open mouth with a mustache

ARTIFACTS FOUND IN IMAGE/SNAPSHOT Christmas Family Snapshot   DATE April 12, 2015

Above you'll see I've entered the six areas of interest I found in my image. This is the seventh step. Remember, the artifact documentation doesn't have to be on a form. It can be written out on a piece of notebook paper, on an index card, in a spiral notebook or in a journal. There are blank pages of the Reference Guide on my website (www.ChristiKoelker.com/snapshot-archeology/) so feel free to set up your own, personal guide using those pages provided or make up your own.

Don't wait though. Start observing and writing down the things you see.

As I've mentioned previously in this book, deciding on the ways in which you'll categorize and interpret your artifacts is a somewhat subjective experience. It underscores the reality of our uniqueness and reminds us that each one will process the shapes, symbols and patterns a little differently.

The anchor on the hat, in the image I'm excavating, is the symbol for an object in the real world of things. I process it as a "symbol" in my way of interpretation. Another person might read it as a "shape" or even as a "sign". I've constructed the *Image Artifact Reference Guides* based on my understanding of the meanings.

It should give you a starting place to match the formations you find in your images to general meanings.

We often look to someone else to tell us the significance of our experiences. I hope I've encouraged you to trust that you don't need an "expert". I had that misconception for years. It slowed down my progress in believing the phenomena I was seeing. I invalidated the guidance I was receiving from my own GUT Gauge.

One of my favorite sayings is: "We're the ones we've been waiting for". In fact, there may be no better way to empower yourself than to believe the messages you see in your personal images.

If you learn just one thing from the process of investigating your snapshots and photos I hope it's this truth: You can trust yourself. The more you trust what you see in your photos, the more you'll trust what you see in your "ordinary" life.

It's a skill that develops very naturally as you engage visually to a greater degree than you ever have in the past. It's a very magical experience and the exact reason I decided to write this book. Now let's get started with the analysis.

1. I found a white triangle created by the light shining on the wall close to my granddaughter. It's most defined end is pointed back towards her. The fact that it's formed from light is especially notable.

A triangle is the most stable form on earth. It implies the number "3" which is best thought of as a trinity. It's representational of the past, the present and the future. It's also used in the spiritual world to represent the Trinity (the Father, the Son and the Holy Spirit). It implies prosperity, success and safety. It's a directional sign and depending on which direction it's pointing, a signal of divination.

I've examined the directionality of the point in this photo over and over. I believe it's pointing in the direction of my youngest grandson, who sits beside me. This makes complete sense to me. These two souls have been connected ever since they were old enough to be conscious of themselves as separate beings. Their relationship, not only as cousins but also as true comrades, continually astounds our entire family with its depth of feeling. White light contains all the wavelengths (colors) of the visible spectrum at once. White is, of course, the symbol of angels and purity.

My conclusion is what is played out in their lives: these cousins are soulmates. Anybody in our family could have testified to that fact but it's exciting to see it captured in a photograph.

2. Here I'm indicating that I found the edges of a picture frame which is just barely showing within the edges of the image I'm excavating. The corners of the picture frame point towards my granddaughter and me. When this photo was taken I had not yet experienced remembering a traumatic event in my life. My recollection of it was triggered by watching my granddaughter blissfully dancing, all alone, at a restaurant one evening. After I dealt with the submerged memory, I was able to function better in many areas of my life. The fact that there's literally a black line between the two arrows that leads the line of sight from her to me reassures me that I'm reading the sign correctly.

3. Yet another triangle is formed by the three ovals traced around the heads of the three adult women. As I said before, one of the essences of what defines this image as a snapshot instead of simply a photograph is that we self-selected our positions. No outside "professional" was posing us. Only moments before we were scrambling around and laughing as my son set up his camera to remotely click the shutter after we had found our places.

Ovals are inherently feminine. Although almost everybody's head is in the shape of an oval, it's often the alignment or context within the situation that will tip us off as to their meaning within the entire tableau. They indicate fertility (egg-shaped) and new beginnings. Along with those more common links, are the deeper meanings related to completeness and hope.

I see a great deal here, not only in positioning, but also in the expressions on each of our faces. My daughter looking straight into the lens with her choice of a regal nutcracker is significant for me. My daughter-in-law cradling her magical, wizard nutcracker with a shy peek toward the camera makes sense as well.

And there I am, in the upper left corner, with my Germanic-themed nutcracker, half out of the picture. In fact, that's what I've had to do over these last few years. I've had to be half in and half out of my family's lives so I can pursue documentary projects that require a great deal of my time. It's been a challenge for me because I've always been a hands-on mom and g-mom. I love to go to all the ballet recitals, read bedtime stories and bake cookies. I also relish the time I'm able to spend with my children and their spouses. Yet I have my own work to accomplish in my "sage-age."

My mother was of German heritage. Her family came first and she turned down a career as a pharmacist to be a full-time, boots on the ground mom and grandmother. I'm torn spiritually and physically between the two worlds. I see that internal battle depicted here.

The triangle repeats again within the center area of the image, anchored by the three adult women of the family. The point of the "arrow" is grounded by my daughter. The one of out of all of us who's picking up the crown and displaying it in front of her, almost directly in the center of the image. Anyone who knows my daughter recognizes that she embraces her role as a leader firmly. Just as she's displaying in this picture.

In alchemy, a downward point on a triangle represents the feminine.

To me, the three women here represent the past, present and future aspect of the number three.

4. Sitting to my daughter's right is her oldest son. I've circled the "anchor" symbol on the hat of the nutcracker he's holding. A hat is representative of the covering of the top of the head. The place where the physical realm meets the spiritual one. The color of the hat is white and we're seeing an actual symbol repeating the action we're witnessing from his mother. He's an "anchoring" force in his world as opposed to a supporting one. The anchor is embroidered into the nutcracker's hat in gold. Gold is the metal used to symbolize the making and/or keeping of a promise (as in the wearing of a golden wedding ring). He's a little bit behind my son (in the striped cap) but I read this not as he's hiding but as a young man who's emerging into his power as a grounding force in the family. His actual personality is adventurous yet stable.

This snapshot was taken two years ago when he was 15. Now, at 17, he's done the work to be one in forty students participating in a nursing program at his high school. In another year, he will "emerge" as an employable nursing assistant and emergency medical technician. He wants to continue his certification but also wants to travel as a nurse. On ships and by air. He didn't consciously know any of this was possible when the camera recorded his image here. As an aside on my part, nurses historically have always worn white hats.

5. To the right of my daughter is her middle son. Although there were plenty of nutcrackers left from which to choose, he chose a Santa figure instead. Without going into too many specifics that might cause him to become uncomfortable when he reads this, he has a very big heart. One might say that fairness and justice play a tremendously important part in his worldview. He's a traditionalist. He takes holidays and family very seriously. He likes to laugh but has a hard time allowing anyone to be the target at which the laughter is aimed. I never would have noticed, in fact never did notice, that he had chosen something other than a nutcracker in our picture. Yet it's so like he to be the one person in the room who broadens our minds to include a culturally significant symbol in the group.

6. Finally, there's Z. The handsome little fellow to my right. He was the long awaited final addition of boys to our family. OK, my daughter and son-in-law thought they wanted a daughter but instead Z showed up and none of us could have imagined a more wonderful occurrence. He's our "golden" child. Funny, smart, perceptive. Z is five years old in this photo. Not old enough to be able to understand how funny it would be to see the wide-open mouth of his gladiator-nutcracker, with the Groucho mustache no less, hooting at the viewer into eternity. Yet that's exactly who Z is! He gets big, world humor on a small, human level. He naturally demonstrates it all the time. Just like he's showing us here.

I also find it significant that he chose a soldier. Just about the same period of time as we met for this Christmas get together, Z started saying he wanted to be in the Peace Corps. We asked him what he thought that was and he replied, "it means you're a soldier to help people." His little golden nutcracker soldier marches forward proclaiming Z's little boy dreams. His close-mouthed, Mona Lisa smile echoes the one on his mother's face. In fact, they share the roles of the family jesters. Both of them can make us all laugh in spite of ourselves.

I plan to revisit this photo annually just to discover how many more messages are lying within it. I stopped after excavating after only six areas of interest for the sake of brevity. And also because I think it's important not to go too far, too fast in my explanations. You can always do more. Yet even if you make a couple of connections to begin with you'll be quite occupied with the possible implication. Sometimes decoding just one, single symbol or sign will set you reeling. So this practice is definitely not about quantity.

I notice there's a message in the striped hat worn by my son and an interesting metaphor as to why he's in a jacket when none of the rest of us have our coats on. There's also a message in my son-in-law's position and choice of Revolutionary War/George Washington nutcracker. I can take the analysis as far as I want.

However, as I review the connections that have been revealed to me during this intentional mining expedition into a personal image, I realize I'm having the same experience I always have. I clearly see—once again—that there's a tremendous amount of meaning in each and every moment of our lives. I recognize that the answers to our deepest questions and our understanding of our personal mysteries are as close as our snapshots. They're waiting inside the boundaries of our photos. When we practice by finding signs and symbols in our snapshots and we to learn how to recognize them in their suspended state, we'll be able to eventually see them around us in our daily lives.

This has been a streamlined version of the more intensive and scientific one that I explained and illustrated in the chapter about working by hand on paper. Obviously, you can take as much or as little as serves you in your excavations. There are NO RULES that are set in stone. My explorations continue to yield new, exciting ways to mine my snapshots. Relax. Enjoy. Use what feels good to you. Discard or file away the rest for another time.

You don't need one more manual to follow. This book was designed as a handbook for the many folks who've requested that I explain how I do what I do. I don't do all of the steps every single time. But I perform most of them most of the time as I walk into the magical world that awaits us in our personal photographs.

Here's an example of one of my personal Snapshot Archeology readings. This is messier than the analyses I do for clients but it's perfectly fine for me when I'm doing my own excavations. I included this example because you don't have to wait until you understand an entire concept before you jump in to try it.

Above, on the left, is a snapshot of my paternal grandmother, Syble. It was captured in the Oklahoma mountains sometime in the mid 1980s but it wasn't taken by me. My grandmother loved to retreat from the city to her small cabin in the Kiamichi Mountains, surrounded by trees. She liked to fish and to generally putter around or cook for her family. Mostly, though, she loved to remember how much fun she had as a young girl with her parents while they were trying to get established in the area.

I was born on her 51st birthday. This quick shot is tremendously special to me for the symbols it offers. Syble was extremely involved with her church in Norman, OK. She read her bible with the enthusiasm of a theologian. The high-point of her life was making a pilgrimage to Israel just a few years before this photo was taken.

For a very long time, I didn't put this image in an album. Neither did I frame it. I sort of just moved it around from book to drawer to box. It fascinated me. But it wasn't until I applied Snapshot Archeology to it that I knew the powerful reasons it had always magnetized my attention. When we look closely at elements of an image that bring up emotions in us, it changes the amount of potential energy available to us.

Historically, a "sybyl" was a prophetess in antiquity. Greek and Roman rulers would consult their sibyl as the ultimate authority when trying to divine which direction to take in war or politics. The image of my grandmother here appears as if she's "offering" sage direction to the viewer.

Some of the artifacts that attracted me are:

I. She's wearing a dark blue ball cap. That would generally be considered symbolic of the masculine. Especially for a prim and proper "lady" like my grandmother. Yet the angle of the cap and the shadows keep me from seeing the bill of it.

The depth of the blue color of the cap intrigues me and leads me to call it an indigo. Indigo is associated with the spiritual world. It's denotes intuitive abilities and wisdom. When I examine it with engaged attention, I see that the cap is darker in some places that others. It truly could be the shape of a crown that's centered over her "third eye". Remember here, I'm referring to spiritual symbols that have been around for hundreds of generations.

Below is the close up of my Syble's cap. Then the outline of her cap I traced in dots in the center image. And finally a close up of the most famous Cumaean Sibyl (depicted in 1450 by the painter Andre del Castagno.)

II. She has, what appear to me as, small white "wings" that are formed by the collar of her shirt. Also, her white hair peeking out from under her cap mirrors the wings on her collar. Mirroring is important in that it reinforces what's being noticed.

Above is a section from a fresco painted by Raphael in 1514 entitled *Sibyls Receiving Instruction from Angels*. It's a small area taken from the larger piece decorating the interior of the Santa Maria della Pace in Rome in which Raphael shows the four sibyls together (Cumaean, Persian, Phrygian and Tiburtino).

You'll notice in the fresco painted above the arch, there are a number of angels depicted delivering messages to the sibyls.

III. & IV. The position of my grandmother's hand is tremendously significant to me. Perhaps one of the truly overwhelming messages. She doesn't have a fist, which might be a more expected action since she's holding up two relative good sized fish. She's offering them toward the viewer with an open hand. And they're posed almost as if she were in a painting by a Renaissance painter. As if she's indicating, "here's the fish I've caught."

I set out on my search with the clues "sibyls painted by Renaissance artists."

I also went looking for what sort of important events the sibyls prophesied. I found one in particular which stood out to me significantly in reference to this snapshot of my grandmother Syble. The Cumaean sibyl figured prominently in Roman stories because one of her prophesies foretold the birth of a savior, whom Christians of that era identified as Jesus.

Upon reflecting about a biblical reference involving Jesus and fish, I immediately connected the story of Jesus feeding the 5000 people who came to hear him speak with the few fishes and a couple of loaves of bread his disciples had for their own lunches. They were multiplied miraculously until there was enough to feed the entire crowd. Is my grandmother telling me/the viewer, "Have faith because there's always enough to sustain you."? Or "Jesus will provide for you just as he did for the 5000 who were listening to him two thousand years ago."?

I am certain, from her life-long devotion to the stories about Jesus, that if she left a message to her descendants it would be this one. Or one very similar.

V. Oddly, hanging around her neck are a strand of pearls. They are real and they were very precious to her. It's incongruous to me that she would be wearing them to go fishing. The ball cap and pearls together are a message. The masculine and the feminine are represented. Pearls are the oldest known gems and for eons were considered the most valuable. They represent wisdom learned through experience and historically symbolize purity and integrity.

In thinking more about their reference to Jesus, He is quoted in the book of Matthew (chapter 7 and verse 6) as saying, "Do not give what is holy to the dogs; nor cast your pearls before swine, lest they trample them under their feet, and turn and tear you in pieces." I might take this to mean that since she is wearing her pearls while offering these objects that are symbolic of faith and plenty; she's sure her message will speak for itself. The viewer will see her communication if they're ready. I didn't recognize it for almost three decades.

VI. & VII. Syble is delivering her message between downward-pointing triangles of white and black: light and dark, life and death. She has her glasses on to see clearly and her mouth is open with the corners turned up in a smile.

Finally, below is a photograph of Michelangelo's version of the Cumaean Sibyl as he painted her on the ceiling of the Sistine Chapel in Rome around 1510.

In his interpretation, the sibyl is an old woman, but in no way a "little old lady". The muscular arms depicted on her would put a 25 year-old body builder to shame. She's powerful and she's robust. On her head is a white, cap-like covering. Just like my Syble, she has elements of the masculine and feminine.

A Roman legion is told that the Cumaean Sibyl asked Apollo for a favor. She gathered up a handful of sand and said, "grant me to see as many birthdays as there are sand grains in my hand." Apollo granted her wish, but the Sibyl had neglected to ask for her youth to accompany her into the future. So she lived on for a thousand years as she grew ancient at the same time.

This is the way in which Michelangelo depicted her: in her great age alongside her great wisdom.

The Surprising Discovery of the Penitente Morada Image

WORKING WITH THUMBNAILS, PROOF SHEETS OR SLIDES

I've discovered some incredible messages when I've scanned my slides and proof sheets on a regular home scanner and then magnified them in Photoshop.

One of my favorites is the image on the previous page. It's a shot I took many years ago of an adobe Penitente morada (prayer house) in Abiquiu, New Mexico. Its formal name is the *La Morada de Nuestra Señora de Dolores del Alto de Abiquiú*. Archeologists date the structure from the late 18th century as a meeting place for the Hermanos Penitentes—the Brotherhood of the Penitent.

This is a selection from a flat proof sheet. I scanned it on my trusty Canon at 800 dpi so I wouldn't miss a single detail.

It's an incredibly meaningful personal image for me because the tiny adobe morada is located on a hill above—at the time it was taken—the house of Georgia O'Keeffe.

I captured the snapshot on a blustery spring afternoon as I ambled along the edge of a mesa-like area. I looked up into the rolling clouds and my eyes moved down to the area below the hill. I'm positive that I was aware of the location upon which O'Keeffe's house was situated but I didn't realize that this mini-mesa overlooked it. Incredibly, just at the moment I was becoming aware of the scene I was viewing, the artist herself stepped out of her front door and into the open-air courtyard. Dressed in her signature black attire, she was headed toward a Mercedes as black as her clothing.

I struggled to pull my eyes away. On one hand, I was horrified that I'd "spied" on one of my all-time favorite artistic idols. Yet I was struck motionless by the gift that was being bestowed upon me in that flash of an instant. I don't think she was aware of my gaze. It wasn't as if I meant to be looking into her courtyard; it just synchronistically happened. A chance of a lifetime for me to "accidentally steal" a brief glimpse of an extraordinarily creative spirit who'd influenced me deeply for my entire adult life.

So that's the sort of latent energy this tiny two-by-two-inch image has residing in it for me. And I haven't even started to excavate it yet! When I decided it was time to investigate the images on this precious proof sheet, I knew I'd be in for quite a ride.

Anyone who's ever lived in or even visited the state of my birth, New Mexico, knows it can be a wild and windy place. Azure skies brushed with streaks of white clouds one minute. Bruised, boiling foams of vapor in hues of purple, gray and black the next. Initially, when I look at the image, it's the sky that speaks to me most profoundly.

As I magnify the image more, focusing on the area within the green triangle I drew with the Photoshop line tool, I begin to make out what's hidden within the ridges, below the dramatic sky and the little church.

Incredibly, within the top portion of the triangle, I can see there are the shapes of three crosses revealed within the dark shadow of the rocks. The leading tip of the triangle is pointing up from what would appear in the photograph to be the interior of the earth. Pointing up toward the tumultuous sky and the morada. In this case, I did lighten the exposure just a little because I began to also see the face of a man, looking down in respect or in prayer. He appears to be wearing a head-piece of some sort. His head is bent toward the crosses. I see other faces as well but this is enough for the moment.

If you search for images on the Web of the Penitente Morada in Abiquiu, you'll find an entirely different angle of it. It's the one that's the most often photographed. They'll frequently look like the beautiful image that you see on the following page. In it, as in the majority of images focusing on this subject, you'll behold the morada

from another angle and like most people who initially approach the church, your attention will immediately be drawn to the three powerfully dramatic crosses that seem to stand guard just past it. Their silent silhouettes present an unforgettable portrait against the sky.

Phenomenal messages "appear" when you "blow up" your images.

Penitente Morada in Abiquiu, NM. (Shutterstock)

The Penitentes are a secretive sect of Roman Catholics in the Southwest who've practiced self-flagellation and the reenactment of the crucifixion of Jesus (literally) for centuries. Some historical accounts report that the Brotherhood was originally made up—at least in part—of former Native American slaves called "genizaros." The allegiance of these followers of Christ is literally as strong to them as a marriage vow. When they promised to take up the cross of Jesus, they meant it in a very literal way.

I can't really make out if the outline in my image resembles the head of Christ or if it's of a person wearing a crown that could be construed to be made of thorns. In fact, one of the rituals the Penitentes perform during their Easter rites is to wear an actual crown of thorns on their heads. The two stories—the one I see in the side of the hill and the one about the Penitentes—merge exactly as the followers intend to happen to them when they perform the Passion of Christ each Easter season. History. Devotion. Earth. Man.

Often very specific symbology of a person, place or thing will show up in a snapshot. This is a dramatic example of that phenomenon.

Scanning Slides

It's easy to scan proof sheets with tiny thumbnail images on a home scanner and then make them bigger. Scanning slides is a bit more challenging although no longer impossible. Way back in 1999, when the world was younger, a generous fellow explained how to make a homemade "backlighter" for a home, flatbed scanner. If you're interested, you can read about building your own slide scanner here: www.diyphotography.net/build-diy-slide-scanner-10/.

Or you can send out your slides to be scanned for less than a dollar apiece. Do a search for "slide scanning services" online. They'll direct you as to how to package up your slides to mail them. Then you'll get them back in a digital form. The world of digitization is changing to become so incredibly streamlined that by the time this book is a year old, just looking for the latest and greatest online photographic scanning services will do more than my dated recommendations.

Of course, as always, you're transforming your 3-dimensional images into ones and zeroes so you can enlarge them with an intent to excavate for the details you'd never, ever see in a million years if they remained forever as little, tiny pictures hardly bigger than a postage stamp.

The more you practice looking; the more the symbols and shapes will bubble up to the surface. And the more you practice connecting what appears to you in your images; the more you'll experience your everyday 3-D world.

HERE'S HOPING YOUR SNAPSHOTS
AND PHOTOGRAPHS SPEAK TO YOU!

"There are more things in heaven and earth, Horatio,
than are dreamt of in your philosophy."

William Shakespeare in *Hamlet*

Master Shakespeare must have been speaking about the magic that can be found after you spend some time excavating your images. Worlds that have always been beneath your feet will blink into existence in your daily life.

You've shown that you believe more than your eyes can perceive is actually operative around you. We don't really need more than this life we inhabit if we invest the time we so often lend out to lesser activities that are empty of meaning and into sparking the slightly invisible into our realm of vision.

When I've explained what I see in snapshots to some people they ask me what's the purpose of staring at your photos to see a bunch of shapes and forms. "What in the world good," they query, "could seeing those things possibly do?"

Then I turn to them and ask if they have a snapshot they've always liked handy. After about three minutes of showing them how to observe their image, they don't ask the question any more. They're too stunned by what they see. They're stopped in their tracks by a phenomenon that's unexpected.

Many people tell me it changes the way they look at everyday life. That's the real purpose of Snapshot Archeology. Life IS personal. The situations occurring around and about you every day matter. Not only to you, but to everybody.

There aren't any borders around us in actual life as there are on computer screens or photographic prints.

Yet, like a film, the microseconds perpetually move past us.

When we steal a shot from the perfectly-crafted slip-stream of time we're riding on, we can witness something miraculous.

We're connected.

Every day. Every moment. With every breath.

To the land. To the sky. To the water. To the universe.

I wish you expansion and understanding of yourself as the magnificent historical figure you are.

It's all there.

Right in front of you.

In.

Your.

Snapshots.

"Photography is a strong tool, a propaganda device, and a weapon for the defense of the environment...and therefore for the fostering of a healthy human race and even very likely for its survival."

Eliot Porter

Sand grains magnified 1000 times. (Shutterstock)

ACKNOWLEDGMENTS

Cover Design by Lilien T. Hoffman.

Edited by David Gordon, Ginna BB Gordon and Monica Dutcher.

Photographic Illustration on page x: The Hubble Space Telescope as seen from the departing Space Shuttle Atlantis, flying STS-125, HST Servicing Mission 4. 19 May 2009.

Photographic Illustrations on page 2: First Photograph, 1824. *View from the Window at Le Gras* by Joseph Nicéphore Niépce. The author standing next to the first photographic print that's survived into the present at the Harry Ransom Center in Austin, Texas.

Illustration on page 3: Poster from the 1960 film *The Time Machine.*

Photographic Illustration on page 8: Statue of the Virgin Mary in a garden beside a church in Oceanside, California. (CSKoelker).

Photographic Illustrations on page 15: William Shatner as James T. Kirk in the 1960s *Star Trek* television series, and a 1997 cell phone.

Photographic Illustrations on page 17: The author's grandmother, Arizona Shrum, and great-grandmother, Beulah "Bob" Kellett.

Photographic Illustration on page 24: Photo by CSKoelker. Quote by Dorothea Lange.

Photographic llustration on page 26: *Zackary's Beach Rainbow.* Photo by CSKoelker.

Photographic Illustrations on page 29: Wikipedia.

Photographic Illustration on page 39: *Shapes in the Pool* by CSKoelker.

Photographic Illustration on page 61: Lower right: Museo de Sitio in Palenque, Mexico. Lower left: Kimbell Art Museum Fort Worth, Texas.

Photographic Illustrations on page 181 and 183: 123rf.

Photographic Illustrations on page 187 and 193: Shutterstock.

Author photograph by Brooks Barley.

All remaining photographs/illustrations in the book are by Christi Saxon Koelker.

I'd like to thank my lucky stars and my good fortune for being able to produce *Focus* under the publishing guidance of Ginna and David Gordon and Lucky Valley Press. The word "gift" hardly describes the experience. With much love and more gratitude to you - *Christi.*

For more information about Snapshot Archeology,
and to download checklists and forms, please visit

WWW.CHRISTIKOELKER.COM/SNAPSHOT-ARCHEOLOGY/

Produced and Published by Lucky Valley Press
Jacksonville, Oregon & Carmel, California
WWW.LUCKYVALLEYPRESS.COM

Design and Typography by David Gordon
Body Text: Minion 11/14
Display: Life, Gabriola

Wood products used in the manufacture of this book meet
the Sustainable Forestry Initiative® Chain-of-Custody Standards.
www.sfiprogram.org

CPSIA information can be obtained at www.ICGtesting.com
Printed in the USA
LVOW05s1248290915

456155LV00001B/1/P

9 780985 665593